WALKING INTO YOUR

Prayers

A

RELATIONSHIP

WITH GOD

DENNIS JOHN EISCH

\

ISBN: 1489597794
ISBN 13:9781489597793
Library of Congress Control Number: 2013910293
CreateSpace Independent Publishing Platform
North Charleston, South Carolina
CanDoFinance - Credit Reports: What You Need to Know – Sponsored

ACKNOWLEDGEMENTS

would first like to thank my wife Rence who has followed the LORD's leading all of these 38 years and has stood by my side to fight against the enemy. We have experienced these chapters first hand together in Christ. Second I would like to thank our beautiful daughters and their husbands; Sarah, Rebekah and Ryan, Rachel and James for their support in the writings of this book. I want to thank my long time friend and fellow intercessor Cindi for pouring over this book to dig out the mistakes in scripture. Last but certainly not least I would like to thank our church, True Freedom for sticking it out with Christ and actually living these chapters to the fullest. You all comprise an awesome church.

FORWARD

If I were to start from the beginning I would have to go back to my childhood. It would go back as far as my first grade communion, and my first confession as a young catholic boy. I know He was real in my life even then. Somehow I felt there was going to be a different kind of life for me, I knew it would include my God.

As I grew into my teens I seemed more aware of His presence and I started to question things, issues in Theology. Nothing definite but I could feel an ever increasing awareness of Him drawing me closer.

Some would say that I was a typical teen, smoked, drank, partied. I was a rock star in my own mind. At the time I thought I had it all, lead singer, guitar player. When I reached the summer of my nineteenth birthday my parents had stepped up the intensity of praying for me and sharing their relationship with Jesus to me. One day I had enough and told them I didn't want to hear any more of that (well lets just say I told them I didn't want to hear anymore). They said fine, and that is exactly what they did. They never said another word, but their prayers multiplied to the point where I was drawn to a concert/evangelist whose team traveled across the US in the 70's.

I won't go into the details but I accepted Jesus into my heart that night and was forever changed. The Lord touched coal to my lips, He first healed my body of alcoholism. Nearly six years later I sat in my kitchen with my sixth month old daughter enjoying her smiles. A puff of smoke filled the room and blew across her face. In an instant my heart was crushed. The realization of what I was doing to her cut me to the core. I got to my knees and said "LORD, please no more." My three pack-a-day addiction was like a vapor in my life. He had heard my prayer and reached out His mighty hand. My wife, Renee was delivered of her smoking addiction shortly thereafter, and the Lord started moving us faster and farther with Him.

We think sometimes that God does not have the right timing, but I am here to say He does. Our lives started a road that as I write this today is a whirlwind of adventure. The LORD blessed us with three beautiful girls and husbands to match.

We grew in the LORD, we worked hard in the church, served our pastors with excellence. We were involved in all ministries within the church, but also valued the act of stepping aside when those we had mentored were ready to take up their swords. Why do I tell you these things? It is my belief, that servant hood and prayer are key elements to success in your relationship with God.

Our girls grew up in the church. We opened our home to anyone that we could. By the time our girls were almost in college I thought we had arrived at where God really wanted us. My wife owned a salon and I was management in a successful paper company in Wisconsin. Our lives were comfortable, with good salaries, a mortgage almost paid off. My two oldest children were married and starting their lives, and our youngest was just about to get married. God had blessed us beyond measure and we were happy where we were at with retirement just around the corner.

Flashing back about five years in 1999 I was mowing the lawn as I often did. Enjoying God's beauty in the sun, the trees, and the fresh air. I thought I was minding my own business cutting the grass at the precise angle it needed to be cut that week when God spoke. I remember as if it were yesterday. There were no kids in the yard, no neighbors out doing yard work, just me. He said, "Go to Texas, go to Texas." It was as clear as if He were walking along cutting the grass with me. He spoke it twice in less than five seconds. Little did we know, but that the words God spoke to me on that sunny afternoon would drastically change our "comfortable" life five years later.

Evangelists started prophesying things over us, and they all fit together like a puzzle. The Lord worked on both my wife and myself. Changing the way we looked at things, money, job, possessions.

One thing you must grasp in this forward and hold it dear to your heart is that we are very much praying people. We prayed about everything but it never seemed like enough. I kept what God spoke in my heart and I prayed and waited to hear for his direction.

Then it happened; in 2004 an evangelist came to our church. Prayed for me after the service on a Monday and nothing really seemed to happen I went to the service Tuesday, the same thing prayer, but nothing really significant happened. I returned to the service Wednesday and I said, "LORD, this is the last service I can attend for the rest of the week. I need answers." The evangelist came by me, put his hand on my forehead, really didn't say anything profound other than, "give him more of you God." and down I went. Flat out on the floor. I could tell that He was working on me, taking out of me what was not needed anymore and adding that which I did need. One of the pastors who knew me well had my daughter Rachel and her friend pray for me. He could see I was going through something as I lay on the floor. They both were walking around me as they prayed and Rachel just slightly touched me, I sat up quickly and shouted," don't touch me I'm not dead yet", and then laid back down. I thought, "LORD why did I just say that?" I lay on the floor from 11pm until 1am; I just could not get up off the floor no matter how hard I tried. When I finally got up a little after 1am I could not figure out what He had done to me. I woke up the next morning with my coffee in hand and stepped into our garage. I knew in an instant God had worked a miracle in my life. I had such a strong hold on material possessions, but God in a moments time had taken away years of the world's grip on my mind and on my heart. The things of this world had no grip on me anymore.

The Lord's power surged through my wife and I. It stared happening so fast. I retired from my job, our home of over twenty five years was sold without a realtor or advertising. One man bought every piece of furniture we owned for a very good price. We were on our way to Texas via Miami south beach. We helped the evangelist start a church and college. I was both a student and pastor over prayer and intercession for the college, and church. I also served in road ministry.

Six months later in March of 2005 we were on our way to Texas. We were invited by our daughter's pastor to come and preach. He offered us a position as pastors of prayer and intercession. We gladly accepted as we knew from six years ago Texas was our destiny.

Three months later we were invited to the senior pastors home and he had a bomb to drop on us. He said that the LORD had said to him," you must move aside and put Dennis and Renee as Senior pastors". God can be the only one that can prepare you for what life is about to do.

Our Lord intends for us to walk into our prayers. His intention is to never sideline us. He wants us prepared for what he calls us to do. Renee and I immediately dug in to our newly named True Freedom Church with prayer, prayer, and more prayer.

My prayer for this book is that the Lord's words help you put your steps in order. I believe in Jeremiah 29:11 and take His words very seriously as I hope and pray you will too.

"For I know the plans that I have for you, declares the Lord, Plans for welfare and not for calamity to give you a future and a hope."

Think about it, if He knows the plans for you, why would you go to anyone but Him for the answers. Every one of your steps is planned out. When you hold fast to a steady, constant relationship with Him there comes a day that you will walk into your prayers.

Isaiah 42:9 says, **"Behold the former things have come to pass, now I declare new things; Before they spring forth I proclaim them to you"**. Now why wouldn't He want to have us walk into our prayers?

CHAPTER 1

Stepping Out With Faith?

Now faith is the assurance of things hoped for, the conviction of things not seen.—Hebrews 11:1 All quotes are from the New American Standard Version unless otherwise noted.

I prefer to say stepping out "with faith" instead of stepping out "in faith." It may seem like a play on words, but one seems to imply walking in faith while the other implies carrying faith with you. I believe this has been mishandled in ministry, love, and life more than we care to admit. I am sixty years old and have been walking with the Lord for forty one years. I am writing this book, hoping to guide you and keep you from making errors in your decisions that the Lord does not intend you to make.

I believe many people hear correctly from the Lord; we just don't want to listen to his timing. Let's go into some scripture and see what some of the Bible greats do when faced with commands from the Lord but do not get much information about what to do from Him to start.

One that comes first to mind is Abraham, and Sarah. Let's go on to Hebrews 11:8: *By faith, Abraham, when he was called by God, obeyed Him. Abraham obeyed God by going out to a place which he was to receive for an inheritance.* When Abraham went out, he did not know where he was going; he simply obeyed God. There seems to be a sense of adventure when people are sent by God but do not know where to go. Believe me, there is enough chaos from the enemy without adding to it by starting before God says to go. Adventure will be there without invention, trust me.

As Christians, we seem to only look and see the part that says "not knowing where he was going." I am not suggesting that Hebrews is wrong—not in the least. It is correct in saying Abraham did not know where he was going. Abraham believed in the will of God so much that he was willing to step out and obey even when he did not have all the answers in what was going to happen and where he was to go. We can have that too but only when we have a relationship with the Lord as Abraham did. God desires that you do.

Genesis 12:4 tells us the key to Abraham's success: *So Abraham went forth as the Lord had spoken to him.* This verse says that he had a relationship with the Lord and that it was ongoing. If we have a relationship with Him daily, we will hear Him as well. Let's see how Abraham does it.

As he and his nephew went with their wives and possessions as the Lord told him in verse 4 of chapter 12, we find in verse 7 that the Lord appeared to Abraham again. The Lord said, *To your descendants I will give this land.* So what did Abraham do for his part of the relationship? He built an altar to the Lord, who had appeared to him. We find that after this intimate time with the Lord, verse 8 tells us "then he proceeded" from there. What do you think they talked about? If you didn't know where you were going, but the Lord—whom you have a relationship with does, wouldn't you be asking Him questions about where to go next?

So Abraham set out and pitched his tent with Bethel on the west and Ai on the east, and what do you think came next? He built an altar for the Lord and called on the name of the Lord. Are you getting the picture? We can do nothing without Him, but with Him we will accomplish things that some people only dream of.

Again, we see Abraham call on the name of the Lord between Bethel and Ai. We can see prayer does not always do away with issues of life, whether in your family or other situations, but the Lord does promise us that He is with us always. Matthew 28:20 says, *Teaching them to observe all that I commanded you, and lo, I am with you always, even to the end of the age.* We can see that Lot and Abraham must separate to avoid further strife between the families. What is so significant about this separation of Lot's family and Abraham's family is the fact that Abraham is totally unselfish and allows Lot to pick where he wants to go. If Lot goes east, Abraham will go west, and if Lot goes west, then Abraham goes east. We must pick up on this unselfishness. We must believe that the Lord is our Jirah (provider), and nothing will escape us that the Lord wants for us. Nobody can take from us that which the Lord has designed for us. We will not miss promotions, raises, or great deals that the Lord has for us. We must know and believe when we have a daily walk with the Lord, and we meet Him in prayer on a regular basis that we will not lose out on anything that is meant for us. Our God truly has our backs.

We see that Lot picked his area at Sodom, and Abraham was then tremendously blessed by the Lord in chapter 13, verse 14. The Lord gave Abraham the land as far as he could see to the north, south, east, and west. What a blessing! So Abraham moved his tent to the oaks of Mamre, and there, you guessed it, built an altar to the Lord. It is very clear that Abraham built altars unto the Lord to commemorate his intimate times with the Lord. It is very clear he also wanted to thank the Lord for His blessings. I know that you can see by these examples that we can do the same thing. We do not have to build altars, but we do need to have a regular time with the Lord. You need to steal away with Him to a secret place, a place only you and the Lord know about. We need to find out what He has in store for us, and the only way that is possible is to ask Him. His plans are prepared, and His will is eminent, but He delights in our questions and our desires to talk to Him about it. When you read about Abraham, you know beyond a shadow of doubt that he communicated with the Lord. Perhaps he did not know his final destination, but he received his directions day after day. This is a concept we need to adopt. We need to ask the Lord, "What do you think?" In short, we need to walk into our prayers, but more on this in a later chapter.

Abraham Promised a Son

The Lord came to Abraham in a vision saying, "Do not fear, Abram, I am a shield to you; your reward shall be very great. Genesis 15:1" Abraham's reward, the Lord said, "will come forth from your own body." The Lord promised that his descendants would be as the number of stars in the sky. Then Abraham believed the Lord. What we must tuck deep in our hearts here is that the Lord *told* Abraham that he would get a great reward and that the Lord was his shield. When the Lord talks to us, we must make up our minds to believe it, wait for His timing, and obey His command. We often fail in the timing of God. His time seems too long for us to wait. We begin to make things happen for ourselves. We believe we need to start it because God forgot or needs our help. People have often taught that our impatience is due to us living in a "fast food" generation, but man is no different from when Sarah and Abraham lived. They had to choose to believe, and so do we.

Verse 3 in chapter 16 of Genesis tells us ten years passed since he left under the Lord's direction and was told that he would have a child from his own body (chapter 17). Both Abraham and Sarah were getting restless. I am sure they perhaps talked as husband and wife as to what exactly the Lord said. What did He really mean? This is the same trap we fall in today. Perhaps it was Sarah who said to Abraham, "By the Lord that our son would come from your body." We put half-truths together and expect the whole truth to come from it. I am sure their customs came into their thoughts and the fact that Hagar could be the one to carry their child, as Sarah was too old to bear children. We do this; we analyze and scrutinize to come up with our own ideas about what the Lord might have meant. Sarah and Abraham did the same and had a child with Hagar. The child was then named Ishmael. We must remember that our God gives good gifts and is a complete God. He is not a God of shortcuts.

When Abraham was ninety-nine, the Lord appeared to Abraham and declared Himself God Almighty—El Shadai—and will most certainly multiply him exceedingly (17:2) The Lord told Abraham that Sarah will give him a son by her (17:16). Abraham was a hundred years old when Isaac was born. You see, the Lord had blessed Abraham with much silver, gold, livestock, and many servants. There should have been no doubt that God would give Abraham a son as a great gift. This is what God knew was on Abraham's heart. Our God wants to grant the desires of our hearts. Our God sets us up for victory and never defeat. We just have to stay within His realm, not ours.

What is His realm? It is simply asking Him every day along your way what He wants in your life. Just say, "Lord, what do you think?"

You may say, "That is nice for Abraham and Sarah, but what about me?" Good question. The answer, though, is simple. Talk to Him every day and tell Him your thoughts—tell Him everything. Tell Him what you think of the situation and ask Him what He thinks. The Lord will tell you. We forget about this part of a relationship. It is the part where we ask Him His thoughts. We just seem to tell Him ours. We just talk; we do not listen. We must provoke a response. The relationship must be two-sided. When we do so, we get to walk as Abraham walked. This is when we actually walk "with faith."

As you go over these two examples of Abraham, you see he went no farther until after each altar was built. We too must not go any farther until our altars are built with the Lord so we can get His directions, His steps, in our lives. Simply put, *work hard where your feet are until He tells you to move your feet elsewhere.* You will never go wrong with this concept. It takes your mind off the horizon of your journey, the point B of your journey. If our eyes are out too far, we will trip and fall on our walks because our eyes should be where our feet have us.

We also see that waiting for the Lord was just as hard for Abraham and Sarah as it would be for us. It did get them in trouble. We just can't seem to wait on God; He takes too long. When we learn to work wherever He has us until He opens the door to the next phase of our walk, we will be in great shape. Patience is the fourth fruit of the Spirit in Galatians 5:22–23.

Abraham didn't know where he was going, but he knew the Lord told him to go, so he prayed and met the Lord daily to get directions. Maybe He told you where but He did not tell you when. If this is true, you do not want to go until He says when, and prayer will get the answers.

Peter Walks on the Water

Let us look at one more example of what we call 'stepping out with faith." I have heard several times in my life that somehow Peter had to have exercised a great ability on his part in some way. If we look at scripture, we see that there was a conversation going on between Peter and Jesus. This conversation should be something we too are willing to do. Let us see how this miracle unfolds. In Matthew 14:25–29, it says, *And in the fourth watch of the night, He came to them, walking on the sea. When the disciples saw Him walking on the sea, they were terrified, and said, "It is a ghost!" And they cried out in fear. But immediately Jesus spoke to them, saying, "Take courage, it is I; do not be afraid." Peter said to Him, "Lord, if it is You, command me to come to You on the water." And He said, "Come!" And Peter got out of the boat and walked on the water and came toward Jesus.*

The Lord answered Peter's question. Why is it when we ask the Lord a question and He gives us an answer, we do not believe it? We say, "No, it can't be." When Jesus said, "Come," Peter got out of the boat and walked on water toward Jesus. It all came together; Jesus spoke. Peter asked, "If it is you, let me come to you on the water," and Jesus said, "Come." It should be a done deal, but our human mind comes into play, and we start to sink just like Peter. In verse 30, Peter saw the wind and became frightened. The wind is an example of trouble. When we see trouble, we can't remember what has happened in Jesus until this time. We only see the trouble. We must hang on to all that Jesus does for us up to the time of trouble, as it should help us get through it. You might say, "Yeah, well, that's the Bible," but I say we have the same issues in life. You must think of the moment. Jesus was there, and Peter walked on the water. We must listen and pay attention.

Jesus is sovereign, and He can speak to us. Several ways He speaks are through His word, which will stand forever. He speaks through prophets and prophetesses, dreams, trances, and sometimes through unsuspecting people just to verify what you already know: God has spoken to you. IF the Lord is going to send you and He has spoken to you, He will equip you in every good way to do His will. He will work in us that which is pleasing in His sight, through Jesus Christ to whom be the glory (Hebrews 13:21). He will teach you faith, faithfulness, obedience, and perseverance. The Lord will prepare you for the negative that will come your way. We all can take the pats on the back, but how about the stabbings? How well can you take those? The critics will tell you a better way to do it but not lift a finger to help you. These are some of the things He prepares us for and why we need to step out with faith.

I would like to get back to Peter for a little bit, if I may. We need to see the entire picture. We left him at verse 30, but seeing the wind, he became frightened, and beginning to sink, he cried out, "Lord, save me!" We can go a little further in verse 31. Immediately, Jesus stretched out his hand, took hold of him, and said to him, "You of little faith, why do you doubt?"

Jesus was far enough away that Peter could not make Him out by sight or the sound of His voice. When Jesus answered Peter, Peter started walking on water far enough so as to be within an arm's length of Jesus. We do what Peter did. We stop just short of the goal—just short of a breakthrough, just short of making it all the way. You see, when we are in ministry and the wind kicks up, we get scared. We second-guess ourselves. We say, "This must be Jesus telling me to go somewhere else. Jesus must be telling me to quit." You want to be equipped for these times, and if you go before He says, "Come," you will sink. The Lord prepares us for the wind in life, for the adversities that can get us down. The wind can be people rising up to challenge what we say and do, causing us to second-guess our lead. I think it is ironic that when we get back into the boat, the wind stops. It doesn't die down; it stops altogether. Why? The enemy has no further need to frighten you when he gets you to quit in the first round.

Jesus tells us to finish the race to win it. 1 Corinthians 9:24 says, *Do you not know that those who run in a race all run, but* only *one receives the prize? Run in such a way that you may win.* He tells us to persevere and have faith in the midst of all the persecutions and afflictions that we endure. Constant prayer (communication), as Abraham did, will guide you. The relationship will allow the Lord to speak daily into your life and keep you going. He is the bread of life, and He will sustain you. Remember when He said, "My yoke is easy, and My burden is light" (Matthew 11:30)? These are the words you must hang onto and not let go of. He said it, so you must believe it.

Peter had a hard time remembering from day to day what the Lord did. We must remember as King David remembered just before he dropped Goliath in 1 Samuel 17:37. We must remember what the Lord does for us and bring that remembrance along to the next issue in life. It is the Lord, and He only will deliver us. We think our talents do it, but the mighty God delivers.

If you are a student just starting college, you should be asking as part of your daily communication where the Lord will have you go when you graduate. You must pray today so you will walk into those prayers at a much later date. Your prayers today will be perhaps in the form of questions, but when you walk into them, they will turn into your answers.

The next chapter will be about prayer, and you are probably saying right now that prayer should have been the first chapter. If that is the case, you will do well. Unfortunately most people go off to ministry without so much as a hello to the Lord. They take for granted what we should pursue with a passion. I wanted to help you see why prayer is important before you move one step. I will share my life story in the pages to come. I have tried the advice in these chapters, and I know it to be true—and yes, the principles work.

David Kills Goliath

We find that in 1 Samuel 17 that David was having a regular day of obeying his father and taking some food to his brothers. What awaited him will be talked about for generations and generations to come.

He hears Goliath taunting the army of Israel. In verse 22, we see that David left his baggage with the baggage keeper. (Metaphorically speaking, we should do the same. When we are about to battle the enemy in Jesus's name, we should be leaving all baggage not pertaining to the call with the baggage keeper. In our case, that keeper is Jesus Christ.) You see, David was about to confront a new giant in his life, but what we must learn from David lies in verse 37. This is what David said: *The Lord who delivered me from the paw of the lion and from the paw of the bear, He will deliver me from the hand of this Philistine.* David, by doing this, took his past and brought it to his present, and the Lord created a new future for doing so.

David gave all credit to the Lord. In essence, David walked "with faith." This happening in the Bible has a fantastic ending. I love what David had to say to Goliath in verse 45: *Then David said to the Philistine, "You come to me with a sword, a spear, and a javelin, but I come to you in the name of the Lord of hosts, the God of the armies of Israel, whom you have taunted."* You see, Goliath portrays the world and all it has to offer, such as the sword, spear, and javelin, but David brought Heaven along, the Lord of Israel. This is what we need to do to fight the world and its issues. We need to bring Heaven along, the living God we serve. David walked "with faith" because he remembered what the Lord did for him, and he knew the Lord would do it again. The Lord prepares those He sends. David actually came to deliver some food, but the Lord had him come to deliver the Israelites from the Philistines. Now that is the God I serve.

By walking "with faith," we have a relationship with the God we serve. When you have a mindset of stepping out in faith, you have a tendency to walk blindly. Jesus Christ healed blindness; He did not produce blindness. Jesus Christ wants you to fully enjoy your walk with Him. He does not want us to be frustrated and experience fear every day, wondering what is next. When we go to Him daily, all this comes into play, and it becomes a plan specially made for you. Thus, "My yoke is easy, and My burden is light."

This chapter was to help you get into the right mode of thought. That thought is to walk with faith in such a way that your faith is in the form of works, so, like David, you can bring the memories of yesterday in Christ with you for the issues the Lord will have you conquer tomorrow. There is victory in Jesus, our Savior, forever. If you are young in the Lord and have no memories as yet, or maybe you are a long time with Jesus but your memories are too old, well, start new ones. Ask Jesus to make memories with you and then carry them with you—with faith.

CHAPTER 2

Prayer

When you pray, you are not to be like the hypocrites, for they love to stand and pray in the synagogues and on the street corners so that they may be seen by men. Truly I say to you, they have their reward in full.—Matthew 6:5

Prayer is probably the most used but perhaps the most misunderstood form of communication to the Lord. I have talked to many people about prayer, and many people have asked the age-old question, what is prayer? "I don't know how to pray. Help me, Pastor Dennis; I don't know how to pray right." I tell everyone who asks this: if you can communicate with people, you can pray. The gospel of Matthew 6:5–13 gives us an insight as to how to start our prayers. We are told not to stand out that we would be seen by men, but this is sometimes misunderstood in the church. This is talking about a wrongful attitude that one would draw attention to the person praying rather than Jesus. There is a need for praying loud at times and in anguish, depending on the need. I think we would have no trouble picking out the person who is drawing attention to themselves rather than praying to the Father in an attitude of meekness. The word in Mathew goes on to say that we are to go into our inner rooms, close the door, and pray to the Father in secret. We are not to constantly repeat ourselves, as God does not judge prayer on the amount of words spoken. The Father actually knows what you need before you ask.

I can hear your question already: So if He knows before I ask, why even open my mouth? That actually is a good question. There are times when we don't even have to speak, but the Bible tells us in Matthew 18:20 that *where two or three have gathered together in my name (Jesus), I am there in their midst.* This verse implies gathering of people in agreement to pray for someone or something, and you would be in better agreement if you heard the prayers of those around you. When Jesus was in the garden of Gethsemane, I have a hard time believing that He was quiet and reserved. He was sweating as though they were great drops of blood. The intensity of His prayers, I am confident, were to their maximum. I believe the Bible gives us an understanding, but prayer with the Father in Jesus' name is as unique and individual as our fingerprints or our DNA.

Matthew then goes on to tell us what Jesus told them to do. It starts in verse 9 and goes like this: *Pray then in this way: Our Father who is in Heaven, hallowed be Your name. Your kingdom come. Your will be done, on earth as it is in Heaven. Give us this day our daily bread. And forgive us our debts (sins), as we forgive our debtors (those who have sinned against us). And lead us not into temptation, but deliver us from evil. For Yours is the kingdom and the power and the glory forever, amen.* Other than this prayer that the Lord gave us, we are on our own as to how to communicate with Him. The volume, pitch, and inflections depend on your immediate needs and how important they are to you for getting answers. The Lord is not deaf, but there is something to be said about intensity and the brevity of your need that seems to push the volume high. An example would be if you pray earnestly to do well on your exam (providing you studied). That would be a much different prayer style and delivery than if you were praying that someone is healed of cancer, etc. I think you get my point. Our flesh and humanness has many, many needs, and our prayers reflect the priorities we give them.

Prayer Posture

What do you consider the proper posture of body language for prayer? For me, there are many. Do you feel that you must stand while you pray? I am a pacer. I pace back and forth when I pray. Maybe you are a person who must lie down prostrate on the floor or somewhere outside. Do you have to kneel? Some people feel their prayers are not as effective if they don't kneel and fold their hands. Some people have to walk. They need to be outside. Scripturally, I don't see anything that tells us we can't be individual/ personal on this subject. I believe the Lord is more interested in the dialog than your body posture anyways.

Many people I know need music playing softly in the background. Some are like me, perhaps, and do not like any music playing. When I first started praying on a regular basis, I had a strong need to have music playing. I likened it to nervousness with the Lord. Later in my daily prayer time with Him, I felt Him tell me to not put the music on anymore, and I haven't since. Now please don't read into this that music is for beginners or that playing music is somehow wrong. It may seem that I am implying this, but I am not in any way. What helps you or sets an ambiance of prayer time with the Lord is great, as this is your time with Him. Remember, your prayer time with Jesus is as individual as your fingerprints or your DNA.

Above all else, we do need to be alone with God even in a group. We need to isolate ourselves to get alone with Him. You might walk and pray with your hands in your pocket. Maybe you are sitting against a big tree or walking in an open field, arms raised toward Heaven. Maybe you are commuting, and you have an hour or more in traffic. (I would suggest not closing your eyes at this time—just kidding.) Maybe you can't find a minute to steal away with him, and it seems impossible to get ten minutes with Him in your day. Let me say this: Why wouldn't He take any of it? We must start somewhere, and the Lord knows we must have a starting point. I do believe, however, that meaningful seconds daily are better than an hour once in a while. Consistency causes regular hearing of the Lord's voice and builds trust and wisdom in what the Lord is saying. When we do this daily, He can adjust us a bit to keep us on track as opposed to using a mighty move to get us back to where we should be. The plus side of this is that the enemy has a harder time tempting you to the point of walking away from the things the Lord has for you when you pray daily. Like most things in life, consistency is key to a great relationship with the Lord. Start out small, and He will help you to add time to your relationship.

Just to help you understand that it takes time and a good relationship with Jesus to increase your prayer time, I want to remind you about an incident in the Garden of Gethsemane. It is in Matthew 26: 36–45. Remember that the disciples had been with Jesus for more than three years at this point, and they still could not stay awake with Him for just an hour (verse 38). Jesus said, "My soul is deeply grieved, to the point of death; remain here and keep watch with me." This had to be serious when Jesus said that He was deeply grieved. You would think the disciples would have picked up on that, but they didn't. Jesus went back three times, and each time He found them sleeping. So if you are wondering if you will ever make it with your prayer time with the Lord, you will. Just remember this incident, and God's mercy and grace will be all over you, as it was on them.

Gideon

Then the angel of the Lord came and sat under the oak that was in Ophrah, which belonged to Joash the Abiezrite, as his son Gideon was beating out wheat in the wine press in order to save it from the Midianites. The angel of the Lord appeared to him and said to him, "The Lord is with you, O valiant warrior." —Judges 6:11–12

One of the most favored ways of hearing from the Lord it seems is by laying a fleece before the Lord. I have nothing against fleeces. Gideon is the example that if our faith needs boosting God will honor them. The point that I don't like is it seems few people listen to them when they do ask. The Lord gives you instructions or a command, and you need more confirmation by asking Him to prove to you He has spoken. When the Lord answers, it is beyond me why you would not listen. We have to evaluate it. If He completes or doesn't complete it, we tailor it to what we need it to speak for us. We are fickle. If the fleece is not answered the right way, we ask again. If the fleece is answered, we drag our feet and request another and another, never really intending to listen to what God spoke to us in the first place.

If you are reading this and do not know what a fleece is, that is OK. You will by the end of this chapter (Judges 6:11–24). As the happening goes, the Israelites are being oppressed by the Medianites. This caused great stress and hardship on Israel. Gideon must beat out the wheat in a wine press. Do you even realize how difficult that is? You need wind to thresh wheat. As you throw the beaten wheat in the air, the wind carries the lighter chaff away, leaving the grain to fall to the ground. He was afraid of the Medianites and had to beat out wheat at night. To top it off, he had to do it in a wine tub with walls. I seriously doubt if we could understand his frustration. Have you ever been frustrated? If you have, at least you have a slight understanding.

One dark night, as Gideon was threshing the wheat, an angel appeared and said, "The Lord is with you, O valiant warrior!" Powerful! Wouldn't you want an angel appearing to you? I know I would. I will say this: the Lord does talk to us. He appears to us in various ways in direct correlation to the task at hand. The bigger the task, the more He will show Himself; the lesser the task—well, I believe you know what I am getting at. How much of a battle are you willing to wage in Christ Jesus? How much are you willing to give up and walk away from? How much noise and chaos are you willing to take from the enemy in Jesus's name?

Gideon's task was to lead an army against the Medianites (6:14). The seal on the deal is what the Lord says at the end of verse 14: "Have I not sent you?" Gideon was afraid! He was not sure of himself. Have you ever felt unsure of yourself? I know I have. One thing I have learned, though, is to ask my Lord the questions I need answers for. When I get answers, I feel surer about what I must do, and my confidence rises. I have heard the voice of God—yes, you heard me right. I have heard the voice of God, but I still needed direction. I will talk about this experience in a later chapter so I can tell you the whole happening rather than just a little bit now.

In Our Weakness, He Is Made Strong

So let us get into what a fleece is. Gideon wants to know if the Lord is talking to him or maybe He is talking to (verse 17) some other guy by a tree. Gideon finds out quickly that it is the angel of the Lord and rejoices (verse 22). The Lord sent him on a project to tear down the altar of Baal and cut down the Asherah poll. We find that Gideon was afraid of his father and the people of the city, so he did it by night. Where does this valiant warrior stuff come in?

You might be saying to yourself right now, "What does this have to do with nowadays?" *Everything*! When was the last time you shrank back from standing up for the Lord? Today? Yesterday? We compromise, sugarcoat, tell half-truths—anything just so we will not offend people. Yes, we all do it at one point in time or another in our walks, but I believe there is a valiant warrior in all of us if we are willing to listen to the Master and ask Him the right questions.

Now the Medianites were going with the Amalekites, and Gideon was asked to fight them both—all one hundred and twenty thousand of them, give or take one or two. So the fleece begins (verse 37): *I will put a fleece of wool on the threshing floor. If there is dew on the fleece only, and it is dry on the ground, then I will know that You will deliver Israel.* So the Lord did it. Gideon asked, and the Lord did it. Now Gideon needed another sign, so he asked of the Lord to reverse the fleece. This time the fleece needed to be dry, but the ground around it was wet (verse 39). God was faithful and fulfills the second fleece. So the fleece begins, and the signs Gideon needs keep going. Simply put, *a fleece is a particular sign needed so we know that this is a task God is asking us to do.* Make sure the fleece (sign) you ask God to do fits the task He is asking you to do. In the past, when I asked the Lord to show me a sign and I put a fleece before Him, I wrote everything down. This way you mind can't play with you, and the enemy getting in there can't cloud the issue.

I want to point out that Gideon starts out with an army of thirty-two thousand men against an army of one hundred and twenty thousand. This alone is worthy of being called a miracle. The Lord says Gideon had too many so God reduced Gideon's army to ten thousand men because the Lord was concerned Israel would boast of its own power (chapter 7, verse 2). The Lord reduced his army again to three hundred (verse 7), while the enemy stayed at one hundred and twenty thousand. Doesn't seem fair, does it? When you walk into your prayers, you don't need the Lord to make things look fair. He will make all things work for you to get done what He had you pray about long before it happens.

> *Romans 8:28 And we know that God causes all things to work together for good to those who love Him,, to those who are called according to His purpose.*

We must understand one thing here. Our God can and will do this for you. He will deliver a city to you with less than three hundred people, but you must be willing to take the time for daily dialogue with Him. Listen to what He will tell you. Stand strong on the faith that He sent you and know that our Lord is the mighty deliverer. The Lord takes delight in His abilities and our willingness to watch them happen. So I have some questions for you. Is He your fortress, your high tower, and your deliverer? Is He your shield, and is He the one you take refuge in? Here, refuge means protection, someone you can confide in and hope. He is the one who subdues the people under you. He will handle all things, issues, and circumstances, but you must have a relationship with the Lord that will allow you to hear His constant voice of direction

When you start your daily time with the Lord, I strongly suggest you purchase a journal or write it down on your note book, etc. This gesture is for you and you only. The Lord knows your need before you say it. We need the documentation. Write down what you ask Him and the date. When you start to document your Godly happenings, your Divine suddenlies, you will start to see how He is there, listening to you. Writing the date is somewhat of a diary concept, but this will let you know how far out your prayers are to the answers God wants to give you. He will set you up for victory, without a doubt. Get in the habit of asking Him what He thinks after everything you request. By doing this, you are joining Him in the conversation. Now wait for His answer.

Gideon had his time with the Lord due to fearing the task the Lord set before him and the uncertainty about what God was asking him to do. Gideon had a need to know. Both types of prayer are great and go back to stepping out with faith or that dialogue with the Lord that lets you step out with faith knowing He is there for you and with you. When in doubt about what the Lord is asking of you, simply ask the questions that will give you the answers you need. God's timing is perfect; ours is not. Have patience. He will not leave (abandon) you or forsake you.

WHEN JESUS IS BROUGHT INTO YOUR EQUATION OF LIFE IN SUCH A WAY THAT YOU DO NOTHING WITHOUT HIS CONSENT, YOU WILL REALIZE THERE IS NO SUCH THING AS "STEPPING OUT IN FAITH" but "STEPPING OUT WITH FAITH"

He is with you every step of the way—when you start as His hand leaves your back and when you are finished as He waits with open arms for you. When you carry Him with you daily, there is no misunderstanding and no darkness without Him right there with you. What a comfort! That allows you to walk "with faith."

This chapter is about prayer and about listening. You must have both. Prayer is easy if you only do the first half. When you ask Him what He thinks, this is time for you to listen. There is a learning curve here, and you want it as short as possible. In your prayer time you want to provoke a response from the Lord, and this is done by asking Him what He thinks.

WHAT HE KNOWS, I MUST KNOW. WHAT I KNOW, HE MUST KNOW. I AM COMPELLED TO TELL HIM, AND HE IS COMPELLED TO LISTEN. IT IS THE WAY HE WANTS IT, A TWO-WAY STREET.

Our Lord does not have trouble listening as we do, so don't put that on Him. We have one mouth and two ears. Let's talk once and listen twice. When you ask Him what He thinks, start paying attention.

Prayer is not about reciting but a release of your heart in a matter. It is as personal and unique as the one who utters it. So make it personal and unique as you can. Prayer at times is not about words spoken but the sounds from the innermost depths of the heart. Maybe this last statement grabs you and will take you to more intimate times with the Lord. Maybe your prayers with Him have only been words, and you can't imagine anything else. That is OK. Walking with the Lord is a journey. If this concept sounds strange to you, that is OK too. We need to be willing to just say, "What do you think, Lord?" Then let Him talk to you. He will draw you in; I know He will. His whole purpose in your life is to get closer to you. He just wants to be asked. Our God is not intimidated by us. He is an out-of-the-box God. He will be waiting for you to let go. Nothing is strange to Him as long as what you do is for Him. My prayer is that you are going to a church that will challenge you, a church that preaches a full gospel and one that will allow you to spend some time at the altar. Praying at home and while out and about is good, but you need the sanctuary at times to gather the spoken word to your heart.

Remember the Lord took Cyrus (Isaiah 45:1–3) for a walk: *Thus says the Lord to Cyrus His anointed, whom I have taken by the right hand to subdue nations before him and to loose the loins of kings, to open doors before him so that gates will not be shut: "I will go before you and make the rough places smooth; I will shatter the doors of bronze and cut through their iron bars. I will give you the treasures of darkness and hidden wealth of secret places so that you may know that it is I, the Lord, the God of Israel, who calls you by your name."*

He brought kings to him. He opened doors so gates couldn't be shut. He went ahead of Cyrus and made the rough places smooth. He shattered doors of bronze and cut through bars of iron for him. He released treasures of darkness and hidden wealth of secret places. The Lord did it for him; He will do it for you. Count on it. Without the Lord, King Cyrus would never have been written about. He would have been an obscure king not worth history, like so many others who have lived. The Lord does this so that you may know that it is He, the Lord, the God of Israel, who calls you by your name.

Numerous verses in the Bible are about prayer, and because this book is about prayers and walking into them, we will no doubt cross paths with several verses in the chapters to come. Know that the Lord is with you right now—no matter what.

CHAPTER 3

Ask, Seek, Knock

Ask and it will be given to you; seek, and you will find; knock and it will be opened to you.—Matthew 7:7

*M*y wife and I pastored an inner-city church in Killeen, Texas, and this verse in Matthew 7:7 and Luke 11:9 was our signature verse for the house. We live by it, and it is real to us. The Lord not only set it up as an acronym, A.S.K., but also a progressive promise in prayer. Let's officially visit this prayer in Matthew 7:7. Ask and it will be given to you; seek, and you will find; knock, and it will be opened to you.

Now, verse 8 explains a little further what it means: *For everyone who asks receives, and he who seeks finds, and to him who knocks, it will be opened.* What a promise this is. There is an extreme catch to making this verse work for you and that is you must believe it, for if you don't, it is meaningless. The A (ask), S (seek), and K (knock) acronym, I believe, is for us to easily remember the sequence of steps. Steps when followed are vital and will bring victory.

Step one is all about asking. This step everyone on the face of the earth could do without any trouble. Let's take this verse and use it. First ask yourself if you are praying for something in your designed will or the Lord's designed will for you. If you are in His will, He will move you to be persistent because He wants you to succeed. Let's look at the unrighteous judge.

The Unrighteous Judge

This happening takes place in Luke chapter 18:1–8. In verse 1, the Lord wants us to know that this parable is to teach us to pray and not to lose heart. Sometimes prayer takes time. We are the slow ones, not the Lord. In verse 2, it starts by telling us of a judge that does not fear God or man. He had no respect. A widow who needs council appears in verse 3, and the judge will not give it to her. She was persistent and did not give up, so the judge becomes weary and says, "Even though I do not fear God or respect man, yet because this widow bothers me, I will give her legal protection. Otherwise by continually coming, she will wear me out." Jesus calls attention to what the judge said by making a statement in verse 7. Now will not God "bring about justice for His elect who cry to Him day and night? He will bring about justice for them quickly." If an unrighteous judge feels no constraint of right or wrong and is moved to deal with a helpless individual due to her persistence, then why won't our God, who loves us, also answer our prayers if we are persistent? This widow would not give up. Why? She had a need, and it must have been important to her. Is your need important to you?

There are as many ways to ask as there are answers. The Lord wants to see our heart's desires fulfilled, but He is really looking for His will being done. I want you to see the other side of asking in the scriptures. We will see a slightly different angle of approach.

The Syrophoenician Woman

This takes place in Matthew 15:21–28. This particular Canaanite woman had a drastic need: her daughter was demon possessed. This woman was probably Greek and born in Syrian Phoenicia. This woman was crying for mercy. She not only cried for mercy but also addressed Jesus as Son of David. She was a gentile but showed deep respect. This is lost in today's society; there is little or no respect for authority. We need to show humility when asking for mercy.

Just to take a sidebar for a moment to explain myself, I have been in managerial positions of hiring and firing. As a pastor, you get to meet many types of people, and what I see in the upcoming generation is a lack of respect for authority. I think the parents want so desperately to be their children's friends rather than their parents. They are not being taught to earn respect and give respect to leadership; rather the parents tell them they don't have to by sticking up for the child when they should side with right and deal with wrong. Why do I think this is so important? Because it caused this woman to have patience and a willingness to pursue. The woman simply showed a deep respect.

In verse 23, it says that Jesus did not speak to her, but it is clear she was persistent to get her point of need across. It tells us that the apostles were annoyed to the point of wanting to send her away because she kept shouting at them. Finally, Jesus answers with the point that she is not a Jew, and He was sent for the lost sheep of Israel. If the Lord would have someone say that to us today, we would be offended and would be out of there in a flash, but what did she do? She bowed down and asked for His help.

Jesus pushed this situation to the limit and said to her, "It is not good to take the children's bread and throw it to the dogs." Oh man, now if the first statement didn't offend you, this one sure would. We would be gone so fast or in his or her face, telling that person what we think of them. This verse is key to why she got her answer. She understood that she was Greek and Jesus was a Jew, but she remained in deep respect and humility. The Lord answered her by telling her that her faith was great. She was willing to take the crumbs. Jesus's words were: "Oh woman, your faith is great; it shall be done for you as you wish." Are you willing to take the crumbs? Verse 28 tells us that her daughter was healed at once. I believe she held some key points that got her what she wanted. She was persistent, respectful, and humble. This is a winning combination.

This is what I call God Math: {persistence + respect + humility = prayer answered}

The second part to this acronym of A.S.K. is 'seeking." In Proverbs 8:17 it says, *I love those who love Me, and those who diligently seek Me, will find me.* This is another promise we can count on. This seeking starts the action of the asking. There is movement in the seeking. The Lord wants to be found.

In Jeremiah 29:13, it says, *You will seek Me and find Me when you search for Me with all your heart.* This is the second clue to seeking Him and finding Him. The search must be diligent and with all your heart. The Lord says you will find Him then.

In Psalms 105:4 it says, *Seek the Lord and His strength; seek His face continually.* The key to this verse is the word "continually." Remember to be persistent.

Seeking should consume you. This involves time spent with Him and does not sit well with the average Christian. We have an attitude of "if I wanted it a month from now, I would ask for it a month from now." Jesus is not the slow one; we are. When we ask, let's get right to the seeking. He is waiting with open arms. He is all about answers; He is all about restoration. He restores our soul as He also restores our joy, no matter what has happened. Psalm 23:3 says, *He restores my soul; He guides me in the paths of righteousness for His name's sake.* Psalm 51:12 says, *Restore to me the joy of Your salvation, and sustain me with a willing spirit.* I could go on because the Lord is the restorer of all we had, whether it be our health, wealth, or relationships. We want to remember as we are reading this chapter that it has an awesome victorious ending. To reiterate, "ask and *you shall* receive, seek me and *you will* find me, knock and *it will* be opened to you."

God math is like this:

Ask + seek + knock = door opened

Drawing Near

James 4:8 says, *Draw near to God and He will draw near to you. Cleanse your hands, you sinners, and purify your hearts, you double-minded.* I believe that the Lord is asking us, "Are you satisfied without My presence? And why do you remain distant when you could have intimacy with Me?" The Creator of the universes requests your presence. Just like any friendship that we hold dear, we must cultivate it. The Lord clearly tells us that as we pray to Him, He hears us, and that is a guarantee. It is clear that the Lord is passionate about His relationship with us. We need to be passionate about our relationship with Him. The Master tells us that if we seek Him, we are sure to find Him when we search wholeheartedly—not even half-heartedly, but wholeheartedly.

Exodus 7:16 says, *Let My people go, that they may serve Me in the wilderness.* This is what the Lord desired from Moses and the Israelites. He desired that they serve Him. You are probably asking what does serving have to do with seeking? Everything. Unless we serve Him, we will never find Him because we must seek Him with all our hearts. We must love the one who promises more than the promises themselves. We must remember the main purpose in delivering Israel from Egypt was so they could know and love Him. The Lord looks for those who are diligent in spirit and who will seek and pursue Him with a vengeance.

We pursue what we value. There is no getting around it. This is a big reason the Lord wishes us to be in the world but not of the world. Jeremiah 7:13 tells us in part *and I spoke to you, rising up early and speaking, but you did not hear, and I called you but you did not answer.* Now I fully understand that this verse is depicting the Lord's sadness about Israel not loving Him as He desires, and there is an impending disaster coming toward Israel. I believe that this verse as I have it depicts the sadness of our King. The one great thing is that we have His loving kindness and it is everlasting, and we have His grace upon grace. Psalm 103:17 says, *But the loving kindness of the Lord is from everlasting to everlasting on those who fear Him, and His righteousness to children's children.* John 1:16 says, *For of His fullness we have all received, and grace upon grace.*

This book, may I remind you, is to get you to walk into your prayers, but it will never happen if you are running the other way. When we are pursuing our own interests, we have selective hearing. We think only men and children have this, but I am here to tell you that all who are after their own gain will have trouble hearing the Master.

To Know Me

To seek the Master is to know Him, and this causes a relationship that binds together verses like Matthew 7:7 and Luke 11:9. Jesus most definitely wants us to find Him, and He is waiting there for us. It always reminds me of when we would play hide-and-seek as children. When we were hiding, there were so many times I wanted to be found. The excitement and the thrill of being found was much better than the boring waiting game of the one who was never found. I remember we would call in the ones who were never found, but strange as it was, we never talked about them. We only talked to the ones who were found and how exciting it was at that moment.

Remember the words of Jesus when He said, *"I am the good shepherd, and I know My own, and My own know me"* in John 10:14. One thing we do not dwell too much on today as a church body is "to know God is to keep His commandments" (1 John 2:3). The reason I believe that today's church strays from obedience of the commandments is the preaching of today is that "we are not under the law." And I understand this. I would like to bring up a point about the Ten Commandments and let you think about it. These are my thoughts on the matter.

In Exodus 20:1–17, we read about the Ten Commandments that the Lord gave to Moses to take to the people. Many churches feel we are not bound to the law, and we are to function out of the New Testament.

If you look at the New Testament side of the commandments, Jesus only gives them two. Matthew 22:37–39 says, *And He said to him, "You shall love the Lord your God with all your heart, and with all your soul, and with all your mind."* And verse 39 says, *You shall love your neighbor as yourself.* The funny thing about these two in the New Testament is that they are direct quotes from the Old Testament scriptures. You will notice the first four of the Ten Commandments are all pertaining to the Lord. The remaining six are against man. So what we find Jesus doing here is simple. He took the first four commandments and wrapped them into one, which is to love the Lord your God with all your heart, all your soul, and your entire mind. So by doing this you will have obeyed all four. The second groups of commandments are those pertaining to man, which is why the second commandment given in the New Testament is all about sinning against man. Matthew 5:17–19 says, *Do not think that I came to abolish the Law or the Prophets; I did not come to abolish but to fulfill. For truly I say to you, until Heaven and earth pass away, not the smallest letter or stroke shall pass from the Law until all is accomplished. Whoever then annuls one of the least of these commandments, and teaches others* to do *the same, shall be called least in the kingdom of Heaven, but whoever keeps and teaches* them, *he shall be called great in the kingdom of Heaven.*

Are you able to see by these three passages that the Lord's passion for a relationship is great, because He knows our success with Him is in obedience to Him? His love for us is in the fact that if we obey His words, we align ourselves in blessings from Him.

As we seek after the Master and as we get to know His word more, we will have a better grip on why He wants us to find Him. I want to tell you the simplicity of it. He is our Daddy God, and we are His children. Even though I am sixty years old, I am my father's child. Even though my kids are in their thirties now, they are still my children. Let me go one step further. Our youngest daughter at this writing is thirty, but even though she is a pastor, a mother, and an awesome wife to our great son-in-law, she is still the baby of her two other sisters. This is how the Master looks at us. We are His children. Romans 8:16 says, *The Spirit Himself testifies with our spirit that we are children of God.*

I want to get one more scripture in here about this before I move on. In Ephesians 5:1–2, it says, *Therefore be imitators of God, as beloved children and walk in love, just as Christ also loved you and gave Himself up for us.* He wants us to imitate Him and walk in love, or since He is "love," we would also then walk with Him.

Knock and It Will Be Opened

There is a happening in the scriptures that I feel shows how we are to knock on a door or what the doors are in our lives that Jesus is referring to when He says, "Knock and it will be opened to you." It also shows how this actually benefits us as His children. The actual happening is found in Mark 5:25–34. I want to extract two verses that sum up when we are actually in the act of "knocking on the door." Verses 27 and 28 tell us, *After hearing about Jesus, she came up in the crowd behind Him and touched His cloak. For she thought, "If I just touch His garments, I will get well."* Two key elements of thought from this woman are crucial in her getting the door to open. Remember, she is at the knocking stage of her prayers. The first key thought coming from her is this: in verse 27 it says, "after hearing about Jesus." By this statement, we can conclude that she has heard about this man called Jesus. We also know that in verse 28 it tells us that she formed a conclusion as well. She said to herself, "If I just touch His garment, I will get well." It was not "maybe I will get well;" it was not "might get well." It was "I will get well." We like the woman must here about Jesus, we must hear the word first, then make a decision to practice it.

She exercised her faith by going into a motion, an action of faith, if you will. She put what she was thinking into a doing, and Jesus opened the door for her. What was the opened door? It was her healing that she received. In verse 29, it says, *immediately the flow of her blood was dried up, and she felt in her body that she was healed of her affliction. T*his truly was a door "opened" for the woman. The reason Jesus opened it for her is shown to us in verse 34: *And He said to her, "Daughter, your faith has made you well; go in peace and be healed of your affliction."*

We also can have these miracles of the Bible. They happen when we trust His word enough to put our faith to action, which only pleases the Lord more. Hebrews 11:6 says, *And without faith it is impossible to please* Him, *for he who comes to God must believe that He is and that He is a rewarder of those who seek Him.* Make no mistake: the Lord wants us to do what we can. He wants us to use our talents, abilities, and resources, but when all we can do fails to get the job done, "He will do what we cannot." Walk with faith.

In the next chapter, we are going into a realm of prayer that I believe will challenge you to the level of excitement. We have learned here about an outcome if we use our faith. The next chapter will take us to that realm of faith.

CHAPTER 4

Seven Seconds With God

Take My yoke upon you and learn from Me, for I am gentle and humble in heart, and you will find rest for your souls, for My yoke is easy and My burden is light.—Matthew 11:28–30

God is God, and we are His children. How do I begin? I know you are saying, "from the beginning." This chapter comes from me to you by way of Jesus Christ the Living Son of God and many, many years of seeking Him. He is the one true God. My goal in this chapter is to get you revved up and excited about praying. Other than the fact that prayer and the act of praying is the most misunderstood power in the word, we also think of it as wasted time, where nobody listens or hears us. If you think this way, I want to first tell you God loves you no matter what you think. I am here to tell you, though, you couldn't be farther from the truth .

I remember the hours I would spend listening to evangelists tell of their walks with Jesus. The hours they spent on their faces and knees and pacing the floor seeking God's face in matters. I would always say to myself, "I want that." I have to admit the "hours" thing got to me. I wasn't getting into that. I want to again tell you this God still loved me even though the hours of praying was not drawing me in; it was taking me further out.

I remember playing videos repeatedly of an evangelist in Mexico who would fast every other day. Now we are not just talking for days or weeks at a time. No, we are talking years—yes, years. I wanted that discipline he had, and I wanted it bad. The miracles this man was seeing in his ministry were astounding and were unheard of anywhere else. But, you see, I was not attracted to the "years" of fasting every other day. I wanted to have his discipline, I wanted to have the outcome, but I was not willing to pay the price. I was calculating the cost as way too high. What I didn't know at the time but do know now is that Jesus was loving me all the way through this. He wants me to "walk into my prayers" continually, not just a hit-and-miss, once in a while type deal. He wants welfare for me, not calamity (Jeremiah 29:11).

I want you to know that I tried the praying for hours, time and time again. I would do well, and then I wouldn't do at all. I would start praying fervently again and then not at all. Are you picking up on my pattern? I would do, and then I wouldn't do at all. I was coming short of my goal—yes, my goal. You see, I don't believe it is the Master's goal for us to pray for hours to Him and with Him and then do nothing at all. I believe that not only with my whole heart and soul, but also from experience. This is where I am praying this chapter takes you. I am praying it takes you to the greatest prayer life you ever thought possible.

I would like to go back to my failures if I could. They are my failures, not my Lord's failures. He doesn't even look at me as failing or as a failure. He looks at a child who is trying the best he knows how, and I know for a fact that He was proud of me every step of the way. Jeremiah 29:11–14 says, *"For I know the plans that I have for you," declares the Lord, "plans for welfare and not for calamity to give you a future and a hope. Then you will call upon Me and come and pray to Me, and I will listen to you. You will seek Me and find Me when you search for Me with all your heart. I will be found by you," declares the Lord.*

We also know that Jesus is with us from the very beginning to the very end. Philippians 1:6 says, *For I am confident of this very thing, that He who began a good work in you will perfect it until the day of Christ Jesus.*

I want you to know that I tried fasting as well. I made it six months fasting every other day. Wow, did I think I pulled something off there. I was the king in the fasting realm at my church. My sweet Jesus must have been shaking His head with a smile on that one. Truth is, you find it is not about length of time as much as it is about dependency. You see, Jesus wants us every day—yes, you heard me right, every day—without fail. Jesus wants to communicate with us every day.

When we started the church in Killeen, we had prayer at 4:30 a.m. at church in the sanctuary every day, rain or shine. It was just my son-in-law Ryan and me. Then it went to just me with my Lord, and this lasted for years. My wife has since joined me now for the last five years, meeting with Jesus every day at 4:30 a.m. Now if you think you get extra points for 4:30 a.m., I think NOT. That could get you into legalism very easily. The Lord is looking for obedience, not sacrifice. In 1 Samuel 15:22 it says, *Samuel said, "Has the Lord as much delight in burnt offerings and sacrifices as in obeying the voice of the Lord? Behold, to obey is better than sacrifice,* and *to heed than the fat of rams."* The cross was sufficient sacrifice, and as we know, the Father was pleased with it.

Let's talk about the actual name of this chapter: Seven Seconds with God. Why seven seconds? How did this come about? Again, I am in a quandary as to how to start. The actual beginning for me was in 1999 while I was cutting my grass. I was just about done, maybe fifteen minutes or so left, when I heard the voice of God tell me, "Go to Texas. Go to Texas." Yes, you heard me correctly. I actually heard the voice of God over the roar of the lawnmower. I can't even remember if I finished the lawn right there or if I came back out later, but I did go in and tell my wife. I was a little shaken but not trembling to where I had to sit down. I remember telling her that that was all He said. "Go to Texas. Go to Texas." We were both strong in the church. My wife and I had lead Missionettes and Royal Rangers in our church for years and helped build the church to some impressive numbers. I had been a deacon and was now an elder in the church. I had sung on the worship team for thirteen years doing solos, duets, special numbers, dramas—you name it. I had a great job helping manage a highly successful paper mill in Wisconsin, earning a great salary and bonuses. WHY ME? WHY TEXAS? We knew no one in Texas, and we never even vacationed there.

My wife and I talked and agreed that if this was truly the Lord, He would make it happen. We had decided that only a chosen few of our friends would know about this, because I had no answers for anyone. For the next five years, the Lord would be gently saying to me, "Go to Texas. Go to Texas." My wife and I continued with life as usual. I am a firm believer that we, as children of God, no matter what, must, "work hard where our feet are." This concept of working hard where your feet are is something that the Lord really wants us to adopt, as it takes our mind off the longevity of the "wait." You see, God's timing is perfect, but ours is not. Ours is selfish, impatient, and too aggressive. The Lord wants to pour into us that which is needed for the journey. Hebrews 13:21 says, *Equip you in every good thing to do His will, working in us that which is pleasing in His sight, through Jesus Christ, to whom* be *the glory forever and ever. Amen.*

The word also tells us about receiving the word so as to be fully equipped for the task at hand. 2 Timothy 3:14–17 says, *You, however, continue in the things you have learned and become convinced of, knowing from whom you have learned them, and that from childhood you have known the sacred writings which are able to give you the wisdom that leads to salvation through faith which is in Christ Jesus. All Scripture is inspired by God and is profitable for teaching, for reproof, for correction, for training in righteousness, so that the man of God may be adequate, equipped for every good work.*

The Lord knows what we need for the journey, because He is the one planning the journey. He knows whether we will make it. He never sends us to fail but for victory only. We just must learn when to go. We cannot take off a moment too soon, or we will miss the divine, the Godly connections vital to the task. You see, our God is so perfect, each piece of our life is timed to perfection. Since we don't walk in perfection, we need His plan to unfold in our lives on a daily basis. I can hear you asking the question already: How then do I get His perfect plan? This is where the seven seconds with God comes in. The actual seven seconds really means nothing other than what I am about to explain.

I was preaching in our church the concept of the time spent with God. I asked if anyone had a stopwatch, and a soldier yelled that he had one, so I said, "Time me." This is what I said, "Good morning, Lord. What can I do for your kingdom today? And, Lord, will you come along with me today?" Time to say this is seven seconds. If you time yourself, you will see that you might not fall in the seven-second category, which is fine, because it is not really about the seven seconds as much as it is about what you are saying. These three things said will cause an intimacy with the Master. Yes, just a simple "Good morning" will start you off right. Now if you are a shift worker and your day actually starts much later, adjust the greeting accordingly, such as, "Good afternoon, Lord," or "Good evening, Lord." Yes, you get it. The real point here is the introduction to a relationship that will cause you to hunger more for Him.

The second thing you say is, "What can I do for your kingdom?" This question the devil hates to the max. The enemy first of all does not know what to do with it. The devil can find no crack or fissure in this unselfish question. It also screams, "Lord, I know you have my back!" This kind of question breathes "servant" and a willingness to please Him, and it opens up many avenues of Divine suddenlies that the Lord has planned for you. It is a question that promotes a reward from the Master.

I would like to take a sidebar for a moment and say do not seek after the credit but seek after the reward. There is a big difference. When you seek after the credit, you will usually ruin your eternal reward, as you are continually looking for a pat on the back. Matthew 6:2–4 says, *"So when you give to the poor, do not sound a trumpet before you, as the hypocrites do in the synagogues and in the streets, so that they may be honored by men. Truly I say to you, they have their reward in full. But when you give to the poor, do not let your left hand know what your right hand is doing, so that your giving will be in secret, and your Father who sees* what is *done in secret will reward you.*

Just remember you have just asked what you can do for His kingdom, so it will not be worldly. The Master always defies what the world says is right. Jesus is the one that is right.

The third thing you will say is, "Will You come along with me today?" Really, how awesome is that? You are inviting the Master to come with you wherever you go. In one way, you are asking Him to come along to give you continued guidance, and in another you are causing a series of checks and balances in your daily routine so the Lord can bring correction if you are to stray. I always look at it like this: I would rather the Lord tweak me daily then to have to use a sledgehammer to adjust me a couple of months or years down the road—just saying. When you look back on what you have said in roughly seven seconds or less, you will see what you have asked is very mature in thought. This is the point: it is not quantity of time but quality in our communication with the Lord.

At this juncture in your understanding so far, of prayer and what it is to "walk into your prayers," are you starting to see that hours spent with the Lord are great? But you cannot start there. You must also understand that Jesus knows this. Your attention span as a child of God is small, short, and usually about you. Jesus is a big, big God and can handle this. We need to know that He can handle this. As I tell my congregation all the time, "You need to know that Jesus knows." While He is totally OK with this seven-second concept, He is saying to us, "I just do not want you to stay there." I will get back to this in a moment, but first I want to address why seconds with God.

The Lord has a plan, and we need to know the plan, period. Spending quality seconds with God is crucial to hearing the daily plan of our lives. Jesus will work within that realm of time. You will allow Him to increase the time spent with Him—I guarantee it. No one who has truly tried this concept has ever stayed at seven seconds. Most of the feedback I have had—including youth, a Lt. Colonel in the US Army, and people of various walks in life —is that their times spent with the Lord vastly increased with excitement. Why? Because they started to see results right away. The Living God I serve will show you within a week that He is listening to you. He will not let you go unanswered. The only thing you must follow to the letter is the three things I asked you to say. While you adhere to those three things, the Lord will cause a hunger in you that will burst forth in prayer that will be unselfish in manner and content. Please don't look at the three things I asked you to say to the Lord as some kind of great formula for success as these will change. It is merely a way to start you on a road with Jesus.

I asked the Lord this question: Why would you allow seven seconds of time with you to be OK? This is what He said to me: "I changed your life forever in fewer than five when I told you to go to Texas. Why wouldn't I accept your seven?" I broke down into tears of joy and awe in who He is. I actually bawled like a baby. I could feel Him drawing closer to me. I felt Him gather me up in His arms. James 4:8 says, **Draw near to God, and He will draw near to you. Cleanse your hands, you sinners, and purify your hearts, you double-minded.** You can actually start to draw closer to Him by spending only this short amount of time. There is one more thing that is vital in starting out on the right foot, and that is to repent. This is a hard thing to do these days. The Lord calls us to cleanse our hands and purify our hearts and this is the way to start it.

I know people who have known the Lord for more than twenty-five years and have no prayer life with Him. When you say, "I know God," or "I know Jesus, and we have a great relationship," and there is no prayer life on a steady basis, I say it's impossible. You see, it does not matter that you have been a Christian for forty years, like me. It does not matter that you have started more than one church, like me. It makes no difference to the Lord what your accomplishments have been. He has given you talents and gifts that are irrevocable. Romans 11:29 says, *For the gifts and the calling of God are irrevocable.*

If you are a senior pastor and you are reading this book right now, I can tell you that unless you have a daily communication with the Master, you are missing the boat. You are in fact, coming short of what He wants for you. You might even be a pastor of a church with thousands of members. The Lord will not take your talents and gifts from you. I know this for sure. Maybe you started out with a great prayer life with the Master. We are human, and we can get caught up in our accomplishments when they really aren't our accomplishments. They are Christ Jesus' accomplishments. We get so busy that we make excuses. Hey! Look what is happening in our church! Right? We need Him! We need Him every day so we can feel the intimacy. In order to walk in the realm of healings and miracles, we need to walk hand-in-hand with the Master.

I would rather go without a vacation for years than go without daily communication with my Jesus. Being human as we are, I know that without a vacation we will eventually crash and burn (been there, done that). I can actually say with conviction I would do it all over again if I could still have my daily walk with the Master. When you are in daily communication, every day has a purpose because He speaks to you in such a way that you know it. You are in the loop, so to speak— God's loop.

Remember moments back I had said while He is totally OK with this seven-second concept, He is saying to us, "I just do not want you to stay there"? The Living Son of God always wants to pull us closer to Him. He wants always the best for His children. So while He is perfectly OK with the seven seconds, He ever wants more, and more, and more, until He has all of you. The concept of seven seconds, as I said before, is nothing more than a manageable beginning. It is the contents of what you are saying that I believe are the key. There is no doubt in my mind that if you are willing to try this, you will be on your way to "walking into your prayers."

John 14:23 says, *Jesus answered and said to him, "If anyone loves Me, he will keep My word, and My Father will love him, and We will come to him and make Our abode with him."* Jesus wants to commune with us daily. If you allow Jesus to pour into you because you are talking with Him daily, you are, in fact, allowing Him to raise you as His child. As a parent whose children are raised and in their thirties now, I can say parenting never ends, and neither will Jesus with you. When you ask the Lord to come with you it is a good place to start, but like I said before He will change things. You will soon say, "Lord, show me where you are working today, so I can join you".

Zaccheus

As you try this prayer concept out, watch, look, and be ready as the Lord will usher you in to working for His kingdom. You will see Him at work, just as Jesus saw the Father working on Zaccheus. Luke 19:2–9 says:

> *And there was a man called by the name of Zaccheus; he was a chief tax collector, and he was rich. Zaccheus was trying to see who Jesus was and was unable because of the crowd, for he was small in stature. So he ran on ahead and climbed up into a sycamore tree in order to see Him, for He was about to pass through that way. When Jesus came to the place, He looked up and said to him, "Zaccheus, hurry and come down, for today I must stay at your house." And he hurried and came down and received Him gladly. When they saw it, they all* began *to grumble, saying, "He has gone to be the guest of a man who is a sinner." Zaccheus stopped and said to the Lord, "Behold, Lord, half of my possessions I will give to the poor, and if I have defrauded anyone of anything, I will give back four times as much." And Jesus said to him, "Today salvation has come to this house, because he, too, is a son of Abraham."*

I asked the Lord a question about this Zaccheus happening. I said, "How did you know the Father was working on Zaccheus, since you would only do things you saw the Father do? I am assuming the Father was there." The Lord answered me this way. He said, "Zaccheus did not belong in the tree. He was wealthy; he could have

36

paid anyone to come get Me for him. The father was already there working on his heart, so when I saw him in the tree, I was compelled to go check it out."

Watch how the Lord will start setting you up for Divine suddenlies that will be for His kingdom. You will want to pray longer; I guarantee it. Remember God math. His math always defies logic, and that's the way you want it. As we go about our daily business as Jesus did, we will see more and more Divine suddenlies or Godly moments like this. They will be duh moments in our days. Jesus will make them so obvious to you that you could not miss them. You will have conversations about Jesus that you will walk away from not knowing or remembering how or why they even started. Jesus, remember, is already there (Shammah). You are the one who will catch up with Him already at work. If you are willing, you will see the Master at work everywhere you go. Your walk with Jesus can truly be transformed into excitement and awe every day if you are willing to just give Him seven seconds of your time every day. Trust me on this, you will progress way beyond seven seconds, as you will see to that. Any fool could see when something works he wants more, how much more a child of the Living God would want more.

CHAPTER 5

The Names of God

Then Moses said to God, "Behold, I am going to the sons of Israel, and I will say to them, "The God of your fathers has sent me to you." Now they may say to me, 'What is His name?' What shall I say to them? God said to Moses, I AM WHO I AM, and He said, "Thus you shall say to the sons of Israel, 'I AM has sent me to you.' God furthermore said to Moses, "Thus you shall say to the sons of Israel, 'The Lord, the God of your fathers, the God of Abraham, the God of Isaac, and the God of Jacob, has sent me to you.' This is My name forever, and this is My memorial-name to all generations." —Exodus 3:13–15

*I*n order to have an awesome walk with the Lord, you need to know whom you are walking with. Wouldn't you agree? If you have a boyfriend, girl-friend, or spouse, wouldn't getting to know that person help you in your relation-ship? So it is with Jesus. The more you know about Him, the more your faith will increase.

Our purpose in life as a Christian is to obey and glorify our God. No matter what you do for a living, you are to glorify the Living Son of God. 1 Corinthians 10:31 says, **Whether, then, you eat or drink or whatever you do, do all to the glory of God.** Our ability to glorify Him increases the more we know about Him. The word "glory" in Greek is *doxa*, which means an opinion or reputation in which one is held. So, in essence, we are saying that the more we know about Him and His attributes, the more we can correctly glorify Him in thought, word, and deed. It says we are to know Him. John 17:3 says, *This is eternal life, that they may know You, the only true God, and Jesus Christ whom You have sent.* So getting to know what He can do, His character, and His relationship to us will greatly help us praise and glorify Him as He deserves.

Psalm 138:1–3 says, *I will give You thanks with all my heart; I will sing praises to You before the gods. I will bow down toward Your holy temple and give thanks to Your name for Your loving kindness and Your truth; for You have magnified Your word according to all Your name. On the day I called, You answered me; You made me bold with strength in my soul.*

King David knew the Lord and expressed his knowledge to the Living God from his own mouth. We too must learn to express these words so we will glorify the King of kings the way He should be praised. I hope you noticed toward the bottom of verse 3 it says, *The day I called, You answered me.* Jesus truly wants to answer you this quickly, and He will when you spend time with Him every day.

Names of God

I am going to start with Shammah, because to me this is an attribute that enables us to walk into our prayers. The name Shammah means "the Lord is there." Ezekiel 48:35 says, *The city shall be 18,000 cubits round about, and the name of the city from that day shall be "the Lord is there."* This name of His talks about not only His personal presence in the millennial kingdom but also His ability to be there waiting for you. His arms are wide open. It is knowing that the Lord is hearing your prayers, He will answer those prayers, and He is waiting there for you to walk into His arms, thus, "walking into your prayers." The key is to learn what to pray for. Praying for His will in your life will cause a 100 percent return on prayer, guaranteed. You remember the things asked for during the seven seconds, right? This is why you start with those, as they usher you into praying unselfishly. As the Lord promotes within you His plan and His welfare for you (Jeremiah 29:11), you will see clearly that His will is far greater than anything your imagination can drum up.

Shammah is my favorite. It tells me of His awesome ability of being there in my past, with me now in my present, and waiting there in my future with open arms with answered prayer. Let's visit some other names to encourage and spur you on to acknowledging them to Him with your mouth.

El Shaddai means God almighty. This name acknowledges His awesome power. Genesis 17:1 says, ***Now when Abram was ninety-nine years old, the Lord appeared to Abram and said to him, "I am God Almighty; walk before Me, and be blameless."*** What a way to praise the Living God than to say, "You are God almighty" How awesome is that! When you can confess these names with your mouth, there is more meaning than just thinking them in your head. It becomes a proclamation. I would like to draw attention to the words, "walk before Me." This clearly means to walk in His presence. How wonderful is that? He is always mindful of us. Oh and one other thing, the enemy of the Living God hates it when you praise Him with His names, and that makes for a great day!

Psalm 115:12 says, *"The Lord has been mindful of us; He will bless* us; *He will bless the house of Israel; He will bless the house of Aaron."* As I walk before my King as His child, He is watching my every move for welfare and safety.

El Elyon means "the Most High God." This name lets us in on His strength and sovereignty and being the supreme being. Genesis 14:19–20 says, ***He blessed him and said, "Blessed be Abram of God Most High, Possessor of Heaven and earth, and blessed be God Most High, Who has delivered your enemies into your hand." He gave him a tenth of all.*** This name says that He owns Heaven and earth (not the devil). He owns it—He is the possessor. This name also speaks about His power to deliver the enemy (the devil and his cohorts) into your hands. This means victory! You surely want to breathe and say this name. He is the most high, but you need to make Him your most high God. When you are feeling down or defeated try saying these names to Him, and you will start to be uplifted by the Master.

El Olam means "the Everlasting God." Genesis 16:13 says, ***Then she called the name of the Lord who spoke to her, "You are a God who sees"; for she said, "Have I even remained alive here after seeing Him?"*** He is inexhaustible and unchangeable. Thank you, sweet Jesus, for this. We can always count on Him because He will never tire of us. There is nothing too difficult or too easy for Him, but merely done or not done, and what a comfort that is.

Yahweh (YHWH) is a name of action. From a verb root that means to "exist" and "be," this name also means 'self-existing one." I get the chills every time I say, "self existing one", such power.

He is a God of redemption and revelation to us. Exodus 3:13–15 says that Moses said to God, "Behold, I am going to the sons of Israel, and I will say to them, 'The God of your fathers has sent me to you'. Now they may say to me, 'What is His name?' What shall I say to them?" God said to Moses, "I AM WHO I AM"; and He said, "Thus you shall say to the sons of Israel, 'I AM has sent me to you.'" God, furthermore, said to Moses, "Thus you shall say to the sons of Israel, 'The LORD, the God of your fathers, the God of Abraham, the God of Isaac, and the God of Jacob, has sent me to you.' This is My name forever, and this is My memorial-name to all generations."

This name at times is hard for us to accept because of the fact that He will be forever. We need to grasp this name and proclaim it during prayer time. Speak it out as you are in praise to the Master. I love this one, and we have it painted in very large letters (I AM) in gold and black on the platform wall of our church. It is to continually remind us of His self-existence and the fact He needs no one to sustain Him. He is full and complete. John 8:58 proclaims that Jesus said to them, *Truly, truly, I say to you, before Abraham was born, I am. I* tell my God this all the time. The more I know Him, the bigger He gets in my heart, and the more I know He can do. There is a popular saying out there, and where it came from I don't know, but it is fitting at this time: "Faith is not believing He can, but knowing He will."

Jireh (Yireh) means "the Lord will provide." This name tells us that He is our provider and no one else. We want to get to the point where we understand that our employers are not our providers—not even our spouses—but God alone. In Genesis 22:14, Abraham called the name of that place "the Lord will provide," as it is said to this day, "in the mount of the Lord it will be provided." Just as the Lord provided the lamb for the sacrifice in place of Isaac, the Lord will provide for you. He is the one you go to for all your needs. I am sure you have been told to seek God's face and not His hand. While that is true, there comes a point in your walk with the Master when you full well realize that nothing, and I mean nothing, can come to you but through Him. This is when you pass to a more adult realization of His provisions for us.

Professing that He is your Jireh is to say that you know that He will get you your job, that Jesus will get you a raise when you deserve it, and that Jesus will provide that house and that car you are looking at. If you bring Him into your prayers as Jireh, you will get the best deals, and you will have God's favor. His provision goes beyond material possession. It transcends earthly things. His provisions are eternal. Remember, earthly things will be left behind, but His provisions for you in the spiritual are everlasting. Do you want the gifts from Him? Are you looking for more of God than your friends have? Do you want to heal and walk in the power of the gospel? He is where everything comes from. There is nowhere else to look and no one else to seek, only Him. I would like to tell you a quick happening that I know to be true, because it was me that it happened to. As I said, my God is my provider and I mean it. I asked the Lord if I could have a raise as I have done many times in the past and to my surprise He said, "no". Now I am here to tell you that bites when it comes from Him. I asked the Lord why, and He gently started to tell me that although I was doing good, it did not merit a raise. He further told me to up my game as that was the popular phrase at the time (He so knows our language). I want to tell you after I was done licking my self inflicted wounds I did just that, I upped my game, and I got a nice raise about forty days later.

Nissi means "the Lord is my banner." He is the one who fights for His people. In Exodus 17:15–16, Moses built an altar and named it "the Lord is my banner." He said, "The Lord has sworn; the Lord will have war against Amalek from generation to generation." Amelek here means "the enemy" to us. Our God will fight the enemy for us from generation to generation. Now take that to the bank, He does the fighting, we merely walk through the motions. The spiritual battle has been fought and won, so all we need to do is walk it in the flesh with faith that it is all taken care of.

Shalom means "the Lord is peace." In Judges 6:24, it says Gideon built an altar there to the Lord and named it "the Lord is peace." To this day, it is still in Ophrah of the Abiezrites. What is so awesome about this passage in Judges is that the Lord was bringing a peace about the situation while Gideon still had to do the job the Lord set him out to do. He still had to pull down the altar of Baal. Remember that Jehovah Shalom will bring peace to your noise, chaos, and battles. Why? Because when you are at peace just before meeting the enemy head-on is when you have the most wisdom. Plus, our God is at your side, never to leave or forsake you.

Joshua 1:5 says, *No man will* be able to *stand before you all the days of your life. Just as I have been with Moses, I will be with you; I will not fail you or forsake you.* Going through life with the peace of God following you is the best thing. It keeps you calm, cool, and collected. People notice the confidence you have in Christ when you carry God's peace. Have you ever had someone say to you, " you are different" and mean it as a compliment? That is Gods' peace on you.

Sabbaoth means "the Lord of Hosts." He is the commander of the armies of Heaven. 1 Samuel 17:45 says, *Then David said to the Philistine, "You come to me with a sword, a spear, and a javelin, but I come to you in the name of the Lord of hosts, the God of the armies of Israel, whom you have taunted."* I cannot speak for you, but I can say this for myself: I want Sabbaoth on my side at all times. Imagine, the commander of all the angels. What is your need? He is there! What is your secret need? He is there! What looks like impossible to you, He is there with His angels! All you need to do is call on Him, and the commander of the armies of Heaven will be right there with you.

I know that in this reading, you went from seven seconds with God to now hearing that the armies of Heaven can be at your side. There is no mistake here. They were always there for you. The question is only can you hear God? Your seven seconds with Him is vital. He wants to speak with you daily so you get accustomed to His voice. The more you listen the more He will tell you, the more miracles you witness.

Maccaddeshcem means "the Lord your sanctifier." The Lord truly is our means of sanctification. We have none in and of ourselves. We need His sanctification at all times. Exodus 31:13 says, *But as for you, speak to the sons of Israel, saying, 'You shall surely observe My Sabbaths; for* this *is a sign between Me and you through-out your generations, that you may know that I am the Lord who sanctifies you."* He is the one who is Holy, pure, and righteous. Acts 26:18 says, *to open their eyes so that they may turn from darkness to light and from the dominion of Satan to God, that they may receive forgiveness of sins and an inheritance among those who have been sanctified by faith in Me.*

Let us dwell on this name fora bit. First, we need His sanctification. We get this by repenting of our sins. To repent means to turn. So, whatever way you are going before you accept Jesus as your Lord and Savior, you want to go the opposite after you have accepted Him. By doing this, you become an heir of His sanctification.

Ro'I (Ra'ah) means "the Lord my Shepherd." Psalm 23:1 says, *The Lord is my shepherd, I shall not want.* He looks after His sheep. We will not want or lack for anything, ever. John 10:11 says, *I am the good shepherd; the good shepherd lays down His life for the sheep.* John 10:14 says, *I am the good shepherd, and I know My own and My own know Me.* We want to realize here that Jesus the good Shepherd hears us and knows us His sheep. This is where you use the seven seconds to its fullest. You as a sheep must know the shepherd's voice. He stated, "My own know Me." This is the reason for the daily talks with the Lord. You may start out saying only those three things (Good morning, Lord. What can I do for Your kingdom today? Will You please come with me today?), but I can guarantee your time spent with the Master will quickly grow. You want to know His voice. His voice will command you daily from place to place and situation to situation. Divine suddenlies and God moments come only from hearing His voice giving you direction as to where it is He is working at the moment given. That intersection of time and place, the "God moment".

Tsidkenu (tsehd'-ken-nu) means "the Lord our Righteousness." He is our sole reason for righteousness. We have none of our own. It is all through Him. Jeremiah 23:6 says, **In His days Judah will be saved, and Israel will dwell securely, and this is His name by which He will be called, "The Lord our righteousness."** Psalm 103:17 says, *But the loving-kindness of the Lord is from everlasting to everlasting on those who fear Him, and His righteousness to children's children.* Romans 10:10–11 says, *For with the heart a person believes, resulting in righteousness, and with the mouth he confesses, resulting in salvation. For the Scripture says, "Whoever believes in Him will not be disappointed."*

First of all, because of His righteousness, His loving kindness is everlasting. It just does not quit. It does not quit for His children. Are you a child of God? I would want to be if I were you, because the scripture above says that "whoever believes in Him will not be disappointed." What does it mean to believe? In John 1:1, it says, *In the beginning was the Word, and the Word was with God, and the Word was God.* So simply put, if you believe in Him, you must believe in the Word, the Scriptures. I can hear some of you say, "Well, I believe in some but not all of them." Sorry, but that will not fly. How would you take it if your best friend said to you that he or she only believes in some of what and who you are? Be truthful. You would be offended. We must remember that in 2 Timothy 3:16 it says, *All Scripture is inspired by God and profitable for teaching, for reproof, for correction, for training in righteousness.* Yes, the word *all* is in play here. You must not always have to see to believe in all the scriptures. This is where faith comes into play. Hebrews 11:1 says, *Now faith is the assurance of things hoped for, the conviction of things not seen.* This is what pleases Him. Hebrews 11:6 says, *And without faith it is impossible to please Him, for he who comes to God must believe that He is and that He is a rewarder of those who seek Him.*

I want to remind you that His loving kindness is there for you. Ask Him to help you with your unbelief. He will. It is His promise.

Adoni /Elohiym is a plural of Majesty. Genesis 1:26 says that God said, *Let Us make man in Our image, according to Our likeness, and let them rule over the fish of the sea and over the birds of the sky and over the cattle and over all the earth and over every creeping thing that creeps on the earth."* It is evident that the Trinity was in place long before we were in existence, to the point of always was and always will be.

Father denotes God's loving care and His discipline, and it is the way we are to address God in prayer. Matthew 7:11 says, *If you then, being evil, know how to give good gifts to your children, how much more will your Father who is in Heaven give what is good to those who ask Him!* James 1:17 says, *Every good thing given and every perfect gift is from above, coming down from the Father of lights, with whom there is no variation or shifting shadow.* John 15:16 says, *You did not choose Me but I chose you, and appointed you that you would go and bear fruit, and that your fruit would remain, so that whatever you ask of the Father in My name, He may give to you.*

When you pray, you speak to the Father in Jesus's name. Why? Jesus name carries the weight of the cross. Our name has no weight or validity. The Father listens as He recognizes His son's name, Jesus. Jesus (*Iēsous*) means "Jehovah is salvation." In John 16:23, it says, *In that day you will not question Me about anything. Truly, truly, I say to you, if you ask the Father for anything in My name, He will give it to you.* We recognize this verse to be true when we ask for things that are in the will of the Father and not our wills. So let Jesus be your mediator in all things.

I could go on with the names of God, but these are my favorites, and they also sum up His glory and majesty. You will want to get to know these names as you praise and worship. The better you know them, the better you will know the One you are praying to and the more confident you will be in the belief that your prayers will be answered. How will they be answered? You will walk right into them. All you have to do is start paying attention a little more. Remember, He has got you as you walk daily out in front of Him. He is watching your every move for your welfare and safety, after all, you are His child.

CHAPTER 6

Running the Race

Do you not know that those who run in a race all run but only one receives the prize? Run in such a way that you may win.— 1 Corinthians 9:24

s I write this chapter, I purposely want to parallel the physical fitness of our bodies with the spiritual fitness of our souls and the spirit that has been given to us by our loving God.

I have interviewed my son-in-law, James, who holds a bachelor's degree in science and has extensive personal training experience in one of our local fitness center chains. He is presently the manager as well. When we run a race to win, there are certain things we must incorporate and some things we must not do under any circumstances. I believe that the apostle Paul wanted us to understand that even though physical fitness profits us little, there is still a profit to be had. The Lord specifically tells us to "run in such a way that you may win." If you never gave it a thought before, now is a good time.

What will runners do to give them an edge in winning? Several things. Let's not look at losing weight as one of them just now, because as you train, you will shed the extra pounds you don't need. Pounds here in the spiritual would be baggage that is not needed, either from your past or present situation. Although it is very important to run as lean as you can, weight will not be a factor but hopefully a motivator as God has you train for the race that He has for you. Likewise, in your spiritual race, as you learn more and more about the God you are now willing to serve, the more you will hear Him talk to you as to what He wants you to drop and not carry anymore.

One of the first things we want to get rid of when we start to train is excess clothing and then get the right shoes. You really don't want to run in jeans or anything with a lot of restrictions. To parallel with the spiritual, the Lord asks us to take off the old clothes and to put on the new. It says in Ephesians 4:22–24 *that, in reference to your former manner of life, you lay aside the old self, which is being corrupted in accordance with the lusts of deceit, and that you be renewed in the spirit of your mind, and put on the new self, which in the likeness of God has been created in righteousness and holiness of the truth.* A runner will wear the lightest clothes possible with the least amount of restriction. Why? So as not to hold them back. In Hebrews 12:1, it tells us this: *Therefore, since we have so great a cloud of witnesses surrounding us, let us also lay aside every encumbrance and the sin which so easily entangles us, and let us run with endurance the race that is set before us.* In this verse, the word encumbrance means whatever is prominent, protuberance, bulk, mass, burden, weight. Sounds to me like something you really want the Lord to take from you. I would like to interject something at this point. In the Christian race that the Lord has set before us, being first over the finish line is not the objective, but finishing the race is. We will talk more about this in a moment.

Remember that in Ephesians it tells us about our new selves having holiness and righteousness? Well, both come from Christ and not from, or of ourselves, but that it is His holiness and His righteousness that we acquire by being His children.

We can see in the end of Hebrews 12:1 that we are to lay aside 'sin which so easily entangles us." To get the true meaning of "easily entangling us," we need to know what the apostle Paul meant. Paul was saying to get rid of sin that is skillfully set around us to prevent or retard our running. Yes, the enemy is skillful in what he does. Make no mistake about the fact he has been around longer than you have. This sheds a little more understanding on the subject of running to win, doesn't it? So in essence we want the least amount of clothing on us with the least amount of restriction, amen? Spiritually we are saying that we need to set ourselves free of sin in Jesus' name because sin will weigh us down and entangle us in such a way that our sin will keep us from running the race to win. We do not want sin to trip us up while running the race.

The next part of clothing we need to examine is our shoes. Do we want to run the race in a great pair of dress shoes or maybe a great stylish pair of high heels, ladies? I doubt it. Let's do this less formal and go with running the race in flip-flops or your best bedroom slippers. You know, the kind with doggie heads or elephants on the front of them. Can't you just picture yourself, as comfortable as they are, running a race to win in something like this? I think not. I know you know what shoes to wear, but I had to get funny and ridiculous for a moment. Yes, you want a good pair of running shoes.

The question in the running field is, are you a supinator, pronator, or neutral? Now my objective here is to help you understand running just enough to perhaps help you know why Paul chose the analogy. If you are a supinator, your feet when hitting the ground will turn outward or have a positive angle. If you are a pronator, your feet will turn inward or have a negative degree of angle. If your feet hit flat, you are neutral with zero angle.

Let me take you just a little bit further, so bear with me. You might just take up running after this chapter. If you are a supinator and your foot turns outward, you will want a running shoe that encourages pronation so as to help you run farther without muscle fatigue on your peripheral leg muscles. Now you may think this is too much, but my goal is to show you ways of running to win.

In Ephesians 6:15 it says, *And your feet shod with the preparation of the gospel of peace.* When your feet are fitted with the gospel of peace, know that the Lord will have your feet properly fitted. Why would He do this? Well for a number of reasons, all being that the plan He has for you means He wants you at your best. In Romans 10:15 it says, *And how shall they preach, except they be sent? As it is written, how beautiful are the feet of them that preach the gospel of peace, and bring glad tidings of good things!* We can tell in this verse that a person who has the right spiritual shoes on will be bringing glad tidings and good things wherever they go. You in essence have beautiful feet because they are shod with the gospel of peace. In this verse of Ephesians 6:15, the word *shod* means properly bound, tied correctly, or prepared. So when you have the right shoes and they are tied correctly on your feet, you will feel like running. In the spiritual, when you have the peace of God properly on your feet, you will know when God says go and when He says to stay because the gospel of peace will be well fitted to you and properly bound to you.

Now that we have some lighter clothing on and we have the right shoes for our feet, let's run a ways. We will start walking. It is always a good idea to know how to walk before we run. The Word talks about walking and not growing weary and running and not getting tired. Isaiah 40:31 says, **Yet those who wait for the Lord will gain new strength; they will mount up** with **wings like eagles. They will run and not get tired. They will walk and not become weary.** When we walk, it is obviously at a much slower pace, which can be boring or mundane and can make us weary. When we are fitted with the shoes of God's peace, we will have the patience to walk and not grow weary of well doing. We will not grow weary of being on a single road with the Lord with not much to show for it at the time. As we start to run, the word says that we will have "new strength," and we will run and "not get tired." This is the anointing of the Living God. It will cause you to go great distances under His authority, His council, and His direction. This is why we want to wait for Him to tell us to go and not go a minute before. Remember, it is not to cross the finish line first but to finish the race.

As we are in our race now, and we have walked for a while, you might be getting the urge to run more. Perhaps you feel like you have a greater wind capacity in your lungs. Maybe you have lost a little weight (excess spiritual baggage) and feel as though it is time, and the Lord is encouraging you to go faster. Let's examine a scripture in Philippians 3:13–14. It says, **Brethren, I do not regard myself as having laid hold of it yet; but one thing I do: forgetting what lies behind and reaching forward to what lies ahead, I press on toward the goal for the prize of the upward call of God in Christ Jesus.**

The Lord through Paul is telling us that as we run we should leave that which is behind us, exactly that, behind us. Don't turn back and lose valuable time retrieving something the Lord wishes us to drop and never pick up again. He does not want us to waste valuable time with things of the past that hold no value to the race set before us. Now if you were running a particular race that requires you to run the course twice, it would be to your advantage to remember what you just ran. This case scenario in the spiritual would be like allowing the Lord to free you of past bad memories and experiences but to remember them only to help someone in the future. This willingness infuriates the enemy to no end, that we would allow the Lord to use such hurts for His glory. As we allow the Lord to use us in this manner, and we incorporate a prayer life that takes us to Jesus daily we will, in fact, walk into our prayers. Why can I say this? Jesus will always set you up to do good things for His kingdom. He is a rewarder and loves to reward. I know this because Jeremiah 29:11 says that His plans for us are of welfare and not calamity. Here, welfare means completeness, safety, health, prosperity, especially in covenant relationship. How awesome is that?

The second half of Philippians 3:14 says that we should reach forward to what is ahead of us and press on toward the goal. What is the goal? To be with Christ Jesus as a good and faithful servant.

Let's say for the writing of this book you have been running awhile. Your race has been for several years. Let's set some parameters. We will say if you have known the Lord for five years or more and have faithfully gone to church and have read the word, your race is well on its way. I want to talk about perfecting your walk, tightening up your ways, and examining them more. In 1 Corinthians 10:31–33, it says, ***Whether, then, you eat or drink or whatever you do, do all to the glory of God.*** Whatever you do, do it to the glory of God. When you are a young Christian, you have many new things coming at you, but when you become an adult in Christ, many of those new things become commonplace or we just flat out forget about them. So the Lord reminds us to do it for His glory.

I have a question. How do you want to present what you do to the Lord? Do you want to give Him average, above average, or excellence? Remember, He loves you regardless, and this has nothing to do with losing your salvation. It just means as an adult you are running the race faster and without stops of sitting on the curbs of life. In Hebrews 6:11–12 it says, ***And we desire that each one of you show the same diligence so as to realize the full assurance of hope until the end, so that you will not be sluggish, but imitators of those who through faith and patience inherit the promises.*** You see, we are not to run sluggish because by now you should have the full assurance of the hope in Christ. In 1 Peter 3:15, it says, ***But sanctify Christ as Lord in your hearts, always*** being ***ready to make a defense to everyone who asks*** *you to give an account for the hope that is in you, yet with gentleness and reverence.* Jesus should be foremost in our hearts by now, which means we should be ready at all times to witness for the kingdom of Heaven. Unfortunately, the way it is going in the churches is the longer you are a Christian, the less you witness. This actually is against what Christ wants for us. We become afraid to witness; we no longer hang out with non-Christians. We don't participate in outreaches. In actuality we become 'sluggish." When as Christians we become sluggish, we get tired. We see our days become 'same old, same old" and then we settle in. This is dangerous to the runner. Remember the Lord wants us to run and not get tired. He will even let us walk but not grow weary (Isaiah 40:31). We are told to go and preach, to heal the sick, raise the dead, cleanse the leper, and drive out demons (Matthew 10:7–8). We need to keep this scripture in front of us as we are running and never give up. If we stay in communication with the Master, we are sure to be in the middle of that scripture, guaranteed.

Let's talk about curb sitting for a little bit. I have some thoughts on this that might make you so mad that you will throw this book across the room or in the trash. Please hear me out, as these are thoughts that I know to be true because I live them daily and have for more than ten straight years. Let's call curb sitting "resting a bit." First of all, why would you consider resting if you are running a race to win? In order to win, you must endure. Resting is for when you cross the finish line. If your walk with the Lord is somewhat weak, when offenses come, you get wounded and sideline yourself while licking your wounds. If you consider yourself a Christian who is tough but find yourself sitting on the curb, it could be a result of boredom and a complacency that is resulting in slowing down so much you figure, hey, why not just sit for a moment and pray about this?

This is where I differ from mainstream Christians. Let me give you a scenario. Someone comes up to you in church and says, "Hey, I am starting this ministry, and I thought of you. How would you like to join me?" Now you say, "Well, let me pray about it." Although, there is nothing wrong with this. I am not saying don't pray about it, but what I am saying is, Jesus has a better race for you. Now this is the way the scenario should go if you are talking to the Lord daily. You see, Jesus does not want you caught off guard. He wants you to know prophetically what is coming up in your walk because they are His plans, and He wants you to know the plans so as to keep moving in the race. So the scenario should go like this: someone comes up to you in church and says, "Hey, I am starting this ministry, and I thought of you. How would you like to join me?" Now you say yes or no according to how the Lord has had you pray lately. If what is being asked of you has any validity in your walk, believe me, the Lord will have already set you up to be ready for the answer. I know this is rubbing some older Christians the wrong way, but if nothing else, ask Jesus about it. I am sure He will talk to your spirit, as that it is what He longs for us. He wants His children alert, and ready at all times like any great father would want for his children on earth, and much more so for the creator of His children.

I want to tell you of a true happening to me, one of very many. I had been praying to the Lord about how I should handle finances and what I do with them with in the church if He were ever to give me one. I had been praying off and on about this and many other things for two years. Don't let the two years throw you younger Christians, because all the while I am praying about this, many other things are happening to keep me in awe of Him (Acts 2:43). My wife, Renee, and I started a church in Texas, and when I entered the sanctuary on the very first day for morning prayer with the Master, this is what He spoke to me. He said, "Pray for my kingdom, and I will take care of the stuff." That's quoted word for word. I started to cry uncontrollably. The tears were so heavy, I couldn't see where I was walking. You see, Jesus knows my language. So for more than eight years now, the Lord has provided (Jireh) thousands upon thousands of dollars for everything we did or needed, from the building of a new roof to ministry outreaches in foreign lands. You see, He told me what to do, which was the answer to my prayers for two years, and when I walked into the sanctuary, I didn't get five feet, and I "walked into my prayers." I want to reference four people very dear to my wife's and my heart and they were faithful for many years to the calling of Gods' voice for our needs. The Lord said something else to me. He said, " you will never have enough money from your congregation no matter how big, I will provide from the outside. John and Kim, Wade and Gale heard from the Lord and obeyed, and it is accounted unto them righteousness from the God of righteousness. Another one of the Lords' financial miracles; One of our four A/C systems failed in our 10,000 square foot building in the heat of a Texas summer. I had called in a Christian man who's business was A/C and heating. He gave me an estimate of $3,000.00, but if we could come up with $900.00 more he could make the other three perform much better. Being true to Gods' words to me I asked the church to up the prayers for children's church and the Lord would take care of the stuff. Early that week I received a check in the mail for the $3,000.00 and we received another check for, you guessed it, $900.00 so by the end of the week we were well into fixing the A/C problems. We were an inner-city church in the worst part of town, so the Lord chose to work miracles with money because He knew we wouldn't stress over it either. I was once told by a prominent real estate broker that our church of sixty or so people does more than his church and he goes to the largest church in town. I have to admit we were constantly looking for things to do in the community.

I could fill this book's remaining chapters with miracle after miracle of what He has done. What is our job as the church? To pray for His kingdom. That is all we do, and the rest He handles. My board of deacons does not question anything anymore. When a new deacon comes on board, they all inform him or her that God is definitely in control with the finances. Our miracles are not only financial in nature. Remember, my prayer was what to do with and how do I handle the finances. So that is the first thing He said to me. We are a church that never passes the plates to collect tithes and offerings. I see nothing wrong with churches that do; I just know for us the Lord did not want it. He alone wants to show us how He will provide for our needs weekly. We have had miracles with alcohol, drug addiction, demons removed, and all without laying on of hands, but just Gods' magnificent presence in the sanctuary. You might say, "what do these miracles have to do with a race". I would say, "everything". Your race starts at your first breath of life and keeps going until you draw your last. Everything in between is the footsteps of your run.

The race to the Christian is life itself, and it is not over until we draw our last breath. Our desire should be to run a race that is worthy of the prize. Our God brings a reward. We didn't make it up. He told us. In the book of John, it says, *In My Father's house are many dwelling places; if it were not so, I would have told you, for I go to prepare a place for you. If I go and prepare a place for you, I will come again and receive you to Myself, that where I am, there you may be also.* What we do in our race determines our reward. We are not to confuse it with our salvation.

Ephesians 2:8–9 says, *For by grace you have been saved through faith, and that not of yourselves,* it is *the gift of God; not as a result of works, so that no one may boast.* To me these verses clearly tell me I do not earn my salvation, but I do earn my reward. In 1 Corinthians 3:8,13–15 it says, *Now he who plants and he who waters are one; but each will receive his own reward according to his own labor… each man's work will become evident; for the day will show it because it is* to be *revealed with fire, and the fire itself will test the quality of each man's work. If any man's work which he has built on it remains, he will receive a reward. If any man's work is burned up, he will suffer loss, but he himself will be saved, yet so as through fire.*

Just in these scriptures alone, I would want two things to happen in my race in life. One is to receive salvation, to believe in the one true God and believe in His word (John 1:1–5). *In the beginning was the Word, and the Word was with God, and the Word was God. He was in the beginning with God. All things came into being through Him, and Apart From Him, nothing came into being that has come into being. In Him was life, and the life was the Light of men. The Light shines in the darkness, and the darkness did not comprehend it.*

Second, to get as much reward as I possibly could. You see, the reward, for whatever reason God has, is needed for eternity. So build your bank account for eternity.

I know there is much more to the race and to running, but I think you get the idea. Those of you who are runners with an ectomorphic body style and who enjoy the thrill of a marathon, you know what it takes to train for it. Those of us, like me, who do not like to run and have more of a mesomorphic (muscular) or endomorphic (fat) body style, it is harder. We constantly battle the run. God is with us from the very beginning to the very end. The word says so in Philippians 1:6: **For I am** *confident of this very thing, that He who began a good work in you will perfect it until the day of Christ Jesus.* You just have to start accepting the Word as truth, start cashing in His promises, and run the race to win. He will make sure you win if you listen to Him. After all, Jesus is the race event planner. Who better to listen to than the event planner? Enjoy the race and keep your shoes tied.

CHAPTER 7

Who Is Your Verifier?

"For I know the plans that I have for you," declares the Lord, "plans for welfare and not for calamity, to give you a future and a hope. Then you will call upon Me and come and pray to Me, and I will listen to you. You will seek Me and find Me when you search for Me with all your heart."—Jeremiah 29:11–13

I would like to start this chapter with a very blunt question. Who is your verifier? I suppose in order to know exactly what I mean we need to clarify the definition of the word *verifier*: 1. To prove the truth of by presentation of evidence or testimony; substantiate. To determine or test the truth or accuracy of, as by comparison, investigation, or reference. My son-in-law, James, sprung this little saying on us while he was preaching the word at our church. We started to laugh so hard, tears came to our eyes. The reality of it stuck with us and has become a check system in our lives. In your world right now, whoever speaks the most truth into your life will determine who your verifier is. It could be a parent or an older brother or sister. It could be a close friend, your pastor, or spouse.

There is nothing wrong with seeking a verifier in things we do or say. Many times, we like that second party's assurance that what we are doing is in fact right according to their verification. What if I told you that Jesus wants to be our verifier? What if I told you He is a jealous God and wants all of us?

This is the seventh chapter, so I am hoping that you are starting to communicate with the Master on a regular basis. You started out with seven seconds with Him, and I pray it has grown because you are excited as to what He is already doing

59

in your life thus far. Jesus is looking for consistency in our walk with Him. He is not necessarily looking for quantity but a high-octane quality time with Him. To pray to the Living God is simply talking to the Living God and hearing His voice. You want to be able to tell Him absolutely everything in your life. Especially when we find that nothing is hidden from Him anyway. We can see this by looking at these two scriptures that everything is open to His view and that He alone is our verifier. Hebrews 4:12–13 says, *"For the word of God is living and active and sharper than any two-edged sword and piercing as far as the division of soul and spirit, of both joints and marrow, and able to judge the thoughts and intentions of the heart. And there is no creature hidden from His sight but all things are open and lay bare to the eyes of Him with whom we have to do the truth.* I want to come back to this in a minute, but let's look at some verification we put up with in this world.

Here in these two verses, the word *judge* means a person or persons who make decisions that determine or settle points at issue. A judge is one capable of making rational, dispassionate, and wise decisions. All earthly verifiers are incapable of giving a 100 percent rational, dispassionate, and wise decision, but our God is! When we use the Word to verify what we do or say, we walk in righteousness of Jesus. The word verifies our very thoughts and intensions. We walk in the funny to the absolutely ridiculous. You will soon know why James had us in tears of laughter with his saying of, "Who is your verifier?"

One that comes to mind is we were working out at the gym, and it was his turn to bench. We had been doing pyramiding sets (ascending in weight but decreasing in reps lifted). He was about to lift 315 pounds. This is a goal of many in the gym as it has a nice rattle to the three forty-five-pound weights on each side, and it usually turns heads in the place. So just before he was ready to lift, he looked to me for verification. He said, "So, Dad, do you think I can do it?"

We laughed so hard that we had to gain our composure. When you think of it, how can my body, which is bigger than his in weight and size, verify correctly what he can or cannot lift? I can only assume from how he lifted the last set whether he has a chance to make the 315 pounds, but then, so does he, and he would know better than I do since he knows how he felt lifting the last set. It is what we do, though. We need the assurance, and sometimes we don't even care who we get it from.

How about this one. This might be more for the ladies. You pick a color for your living room wall. You have spent perhaps days on matching it to a color in your sofa or drapes. You have brought the material to the paint shop and talked it over with the professional at the store. You finally make your choice and purchase the right amount to paint the walls a good two coats. You are now into painting your second or third wall and your friend comes over. Yes, you guessed it. You are absolutely compelled to ask the verifying question: So, do you think the color will match the sofa and drapes? Yes, you did it. You asked the question, but chances are, the person you asked doesn't even know her colors. She wouldn't know drape material from sackcloth. What if she said no? What if she can't see any match whatsoever? Would you stop and redo the whole process? No, you wouldn't. You better not.

This is why we always ask someone who has no clue to verify something we already know the right answer to. We just need that assurance, be it right or wrong, and we will ask the question. Jesus wants us to ask the question to Him.

A part of the definition of a verifier is one who knows the truth by way of proof, one who has evidence or testimony. Who better to have all this than Jesus? It says in John 1:1–5, *In the beginning was the Word, and the Word was with God, and the Word was God. He was in the beginning with God. All things came into being through Him, and Apart From Him, nothing came into being that has come into being. In Him was life, and the life was the Light of men. The Light shines in the darkness, and the darkness did not comprehend it.* Later on in the same book of John 14:6, it says Jesus said, *I am the way, and the truth, and the life; no one comes to the Father but through Me.*

How much more verification do we need other than to hear Jesus speak it Himself? We need to know and understand that if we believe in Christ, we will do great works. He then will be our verifier. We need to learn that we can take everything and anything to Him in prayer. Back in the beginning scripture, it said, "but all things are open and lay bare to the eyes of Him with whom we have to do the truth." We really need to know that we can talk to Him about anything, no matter how vile or how ashamed we are of it. In John 14:12–14, it says, *Truly, truly, I say to you, he who believes in Me, the works that I do, he will do also, and greater works than these he will do; because I go to the Father. Whatever you ask in My name, that will I do, so that the Father may be glorified in the Son. If you ask Me anything in My name, I will do it.*

What we must always know is this: our God wants to be involved with everything we do. Whether choosing a paint color, a car, a home, or any ministry, He wants to be right there. Everything we do and have done is important to Him. I know this because Jeremiah 29:11 says He has a plan for me, and it is a plan of good.

When we ask for things in His name, it means just that, His name. If you bring this verse to yourself and the people around you, it would mean something like this: if we were to build a house for ourselves, we do not have to ask anyone's ideas, and we do not need permission from anyone. The style of the house, whether it would be of brick, wood, or stone, is solely up to you. You pick the colors, the window style, and the treatments. You pick the flooring, the hardware, and the plumbing and lighting fixtures. The only thing that stops you from doing what you want is your pocketbook.

If we were to build a house in Jesus' name, we need to know His every like and dislike. Even though we are doing the work, we still need to know His every wish. Our ministries might even bear our last names, but we really do not get to pick anything. Since we are building in His name, everything must be built to His specs. The more we communicate to the Master with this thought process, the more we will walk into our prayers. Yes, but doesn't it say in the scriptures, "a wise man who built his house on the rock"? *Therefore everyone who hears these words of Mine and acts on them, may be compared to a wise man who built his house on the rock. And the rain fell, and the floods came, and the winds blew and slammed against that house, and yet it did not fall, for it had been founded on the rock. Matthew 7:24-25*

In these two scriptures, it tells us that you would be a wise person if you build on the rock. The word *his* here means you take ownership. I remember a hard boss that I had years ago. His saying when we left the meeting was, "It may be my idea, but you better own it." Our God is love, and He is full of grace, but the Word teaches us that it must be done His way. In John 5:30 it says, *I can do nothing on My own initiative. As I hear, I judge, and My judgment is just, because I do not seek My own will, but the will of Him who sent Me.*

If Jesus did not seek His own will, but only that of the Father, I believe we need to use Jesus as our verifier. We need to pray to Him, and we need to read the Word so we know truth. When we do this, it will set us on a course of true freedom. *He who rejects Me and does not receive My sayings has one who judges him: the word I spoke is what will judge him at the last day.* says, *If you continue in My word, then you are truly disciples of Mine, and you will know the truth, and the truth will make you free. John 12:48, John 8:31*

The key here is to continue in His Word. It says that if we continue in His Word, we will be disciples. It is true to say as well that if we do not continue in His Word, we are not His disciples. In John 14:14, it says, *If you ask Me anything in My name, I will do* it.

We need to walk into our prayers here because He sent us. We were sent because we read the Word, listen to Him, and communicate with Him through prayer. It is a guarantee by His word that if we read the word and pray to Him daily to find out His plan, all of our prayers will be answered because it is His promise and because He is our verifier of what we are to do and where we are to go, and what we are to say.

If you are a baby Christian and all this stuff seems so new and perhaps overwhelming, please do not worry. The Lord has a path just for you at a speed that you can handle. When you want more, all you have to do is ask (Matthew 7:7). If you are an older Christian and you are learning to incorporate some of these scriptures, the Lord will take you on a journey that will rock your world in a great way. Perhaps you are a seasoned Christian and you once saw these moves of God, but you are not seeing them now or at best you only see them once in a while . Remember God's grace. Return to your first love, Jesus, and you will be right back in the race. The Lord will be getting you back up to the speed you left off at, and then beyond.

The Lord gave me a vision back in 2011 for our church. The vision was of a target. The target had one bull's-eye of red. The rest of the vision was of white as far as my eyes could see. I asked the Lord what it meant. He said, "The red is your target and nothing else matters. You must hit the target." I asked Him what the targets were. He said, "Love, joy, peace…" In Galatians 5:22–23, it says, *But the fruit of the Spirit is love, joy, peace, patience, kindness, goodness, faithfulness, gentleness, self-control; against such things there is no law.* So if we live by the Spirit, let us also walk by the Spirit. Galatians 5:25

He proceeded to say that we must forgive. That forgiveness was in fact a target that we must hit. Matthew 6:14–15 says, *For if you forgive others for their transgressions, your Heavenly Father will also forgive you. But if you do not forgive others, then your Father will not forgive your transgressions.* In general, we must fulfill His word to witness and present the gospel in power for His kingdom. Matthew 10:7–8 says, *And as you go, preach, saying, "The kingdom of Heaven is at hand." Heal the sick, raise the dead, cleanse the lepers, cast out demons. Freely you received, freely give.* In short, the Word will tell us His targets for us to hit.

So I asked Him what all the white was about. He told me it was His grace. As far as my eyes could see was white. His grace is the same. His grace goes on and on John 1:16–17 says, *For of His fullness we have all received, and grace upon grace. For the Law was given through Moses; grace and truth was realized through Jesus Christ.* Grace is not a target. Grace is there when we miss our target, but you don't stop there and say, "Oh well, I tried." You pick yourself back up and try again, because grace is there for us. It is not a license to sin or a license to quit. So we failed. This should not retard, inhibit, or stop us from running the race to win. Grace will verify that we tried, and perhaps missed, but grace is also there for us to try again. It does not matter how badly we missed the target, either, as His grace is sufficient for our needs. 2 Corinthians 12:9 says, *And He has said to me, "My grace is sufficient for you, for power is perfected in weakness." Most gladly, therefore, I will rather boast about my weaknesses, so that the power of Christ may dwell in me.*

What a mighty God we serve. I hope and pray that you can see now that you need Jesus as your verifier. You need His mighty scriptures, the living word, to give you guidance and structure. You see, all, and I do mean all, your answers are in His word. What an awesome verification.

The purpose of your life is to have a life of purpose. Let Jesus move you to do. James 1:22 says, *But prove yourselves doers of the word, and not merely hearers who delude themselves.* Let God verify in your life on a daily basis. Under no circumstances allow the enemy to be a verifier in your life. He is a liar who comes only to steal, kill, and destroy. Think about this. Why would you listen to a liar for verification? Listen only to Him who brings life and life more abundantly. ***The thief comes only to steal and kill and destroy; I came that they may have life, and have*** it ***abundantly*** (John 10:10). As I said earlier we will grab a verifier just to tell us what we want to hear. It may not be correct, but we want to hear what we already know they will tell us. Why, when the true verifier is watching your every move and is actually walking with you every step of the way. I need you to trust me on something. When you talk with Jesus He is waiting for you to tell Him the whole truth and nothing but the truth, so He can start to purify you, and put you in line for blessings. The key here is; do not leave any detail out of what is on your heart.

What Do You Smell Like?

When He had taken the book, the four living creatures and the twenty-four elders fell down before the Lamb, each one holding a harp and golden bowls full of incense, which are the prayers of the saints.—Revelations 5:8

Another angel came and stood at the altar, holding a golden censer, and much incense was given to him, so that he might add it to the prayers of all the saints on the golden altar which was before the throne. And the smoke of the incense, with the prayers of the saints, went up before God out of the angel's hand.—Revelations 8:3–3

*W*e acquire a smell by the prayers that go up from us. The Lord knows how each one of us smells like more than I know the smells of each one of my grandbabies. We need to ask ourselves, "What do I smell like to the Lord?"

We all understand the sense of smell. I have a couple of friends who have lost their senses of smell completely, but they still understand its individuality. Women have their perfumes, and men have their colognes. Each one is to attract the other and/or to portray how one wishes to be noticed in the sensory of smell. When I wear cologne, I use one that will attract my wife to me. I want to wear what pleases her, not someone else.

There is a proper way of putting on a cologne or perfume, and there is a wrong way. First and foremost, we do not put it on a dirty body. Even when you clean your body, you want to use a neutral, no-scent soap to allow the true smell of your cologne or perfume to go forth. You want to create the pure smell and not mix it with fragrant soap residue.

There are different fragrance bases, such as flowery, spice, citrus, etc. Each base type appeals to different people. Each base is unique in itself.

I believe with all my heart that fragrances are paramount to our Lord. I believe through scripture that incenses are very important to the King of kings. I believe and will show you in scripture that the Lord of lords knows you by your scent from prayer or your smell from no prayer at all.

There are things that we can take into ourselves that will taint and change the smell of our prayers. We can take on pride or bitterness. To be critical or judgmental and carry a bad attitude will absolutely change the scent of your prayers. These will ruin the fragrant scent. Unforgiveness will block the scent completely. In Matthew it says, *For if you forgive others for their transgressions, your Heavenly Father will also forgive you. But if you do not forgive others, then your Father will not forgive your transgressions.* This is critical to understand, that to forgive is crucial to our relationship with Jesus. To forgive is essential to our scents. To forgive allows our fragrance to go up to the Lord pure. When we forgive, the act of true forgiveness abolishes pride. True forgiveness uproots bitterness and causes jealousy to disappear. When you forgive, you banish judgment on others, and your attitude is one that now pleases God. In essence, we stop trying to cover our dirty bodies with cologne or perfume. We stop being critical of others because our heart is that of the Lord's. When we ask forgiveness of our sins, we are then released from them in the New American Standard Bible. In the New King James Version, it says we are washed clean: *And from Jesus Christ, the faithful witness, the firstborn of the dead, and the ruler of the kings of the earth. To Him who loves us and released us from our sins by His blood* (Revelations 1:5).

In 1 John 1:9, it says, *If we confess our sins, He is faithful and righteous to forgive us our sins and to cleanse us from all unrighteousness.*

When we read Acts 10:1–4, we find out that Cornelius was not only heard by the Lord, but also smelled very good to the Living God. Verse 4: *And fixing his gaze on Him and being much alarmed, he said, "What is it, Lord?" And He said to him, "Your prayers and alms have ascended as a memorial before God."*

The word *memorial* tells us that the Lord liked the smell of Cornelius very much. If you visit Leviticus 2:2, you will see why: *He shall then bring it to Aaron's sons the priests and shall take from it his handful of its fine flour and of its oil with all its frankincense. And the priest shall offer* it *up in smoke* as *its memorial portion on the altar, an offering by fire of a soothing aroma to the Lord."* In this verse, the word *soothing* means tranquilizing, calming. What a fragrance to be unto the Lord. You might be thinking that you could never be that to the Lord. Maybe you think it is unattainable, out of sight for you. The word says it is attainable and very possible for each of us. Let's take a closer look at how this sent went up to the Lord and why.

We see that Cornelius was perhaps a man's man, strong, a centurion who commanded many men. The word says that he feared God. Because he feared God, we know that he was also a wise man. Proverbs 9:10 says, *The fear of the Lord is the beginning of wisdom, and the knowledge of the Holy One is understanding.* We know that he was a giver of alms to the Jewish people (alms are donations to the poor, not necessarily in, through, or from a church). Cornelius was also a devout (Godly, dutiful) man who prayed continually. It does not tell us how long he prayed, although he did go to the temple to pray. I believe the word continually suggests consistency on Cornelius's part.

Jesus wants us to walk into our prayers on a continual basis, and Cornelius is no exception. The word says (verse 3) it was the ninth hour when he had a vision. To clarify this we need to know that that would be 3 p.m. and was the time of prayer called "incense." I do not believe this is coincidental, but very deliberate on the Lords' part. When we give, it is a good aroma to the Lord. The apostle Paul speaks of the Philippians, who gave him a monetary gift that resulted in a fragrant aroma, acceptable, and well pleasing to the Lord. Philippians 4:18 says, *But I have received everything in full and have an abundance; I am amply supplied, having received from Epaphroditus what you have sent, a fragrant aroma, an acceptable sacrifice, well-pleasing to God.* Everything written in these pages is attainable for anyone. The Lord is looking for consistency in prayer (communication) time with Him, and He only asks you to give out of what you have. Proverbs 3:9–10 says, *Honor the Lord from your wealth and from the first of all your produce, so your barns will be filled with plenty And your vats will overflow with new wine.*

When we give to the kingdom of God, we are telling the Lord how important we feel it is to further His work, and He will bless us with plenty.

We are very sure that Cornelius gave without caring if he ever got it back. In Acts 10:2, we see his alms went to the Jewish people. Now Cornelius was not a Jew but followed Jewish practices (proselyte). There would be no way that Cornelius, being a gentile, would ever get a dime back or even thanked from a Jew. When we are givers to people who cannot pay us back, we are most pleasing to Jesus. What, may I ask, could the enemy do with that? When we put ourselves in position to infuriate the enemy and please the Living God, we put ourselves on the path of God's blessings, which the enemy cannot steal. This is why Cornelius was set up by the Lord for victory in verses 5–48, and we find that those who fear Him and do right are blessed: ***But in every nation the man who fears Him and does what is right is welcome to Him.***

Jesus wants us to walk into our prayers. He will cause us to pray for people, things, etc. and then will cause us to walk right into what He has mightily prepared for us.

When we walk in Christ, we bring with us a sweet aroma. Now people may not say to you outright that they can smell Jesus on you, but the scriptures sure tell us that we can have a 'sweet aroma," which is the smell of life, or we can have a smell of death. It says in 2 Corinthians 2:14–16: "But thanks be to God, who always leads us in triumph in Christ, and manifests through us the sweet aroma of the knowledge of Him in every place. For we are a fragrance of Christ to God among those who are being saved and among those who are perishing; to the one an aroma from death to death, to the other an aroma from life to life. And who is adequate for these things?"

I want to carry a fragrance of a sweet aroma of life, and I believe you do as well. Two of the best things you can do as a new, young, or seasoned Christian is pray and be a generous giver. The enemy of the Living God does not know what to do or how to come against these when done in an unselfish manner.

In Ephesians 5:1–2 it says, ***Therefore be imitators of God, as beloved children, and walk in love, just as Christ also loved you and gave Himself up for us, an offering and a sacrifice to God as a fragrant aroma.*** We are to imitate Christ because we are His children. We are to walk in love, which is the first of the nine fruits of the Spirit (Galatians5:22–23). Love being first is no coincidence. Without love, we have nothing. Without love, we are just a bunch of bad noise, like "a noisy gong or a clanging cymbal" (1 Corinthians 13:1). I know that in 1 Samuel 15:22 it says, *Behold, to obey is better than sacrifice,* and here in Ephesians 5:2, it says that *He offered Himself as a sacrifice.*

Do not be confused here if you are a young Christian. Jesus' body was the sacrifice through obedience to the Father and was done out of agape (Christ like) love. It was, in fact, a fragrant aroma to the Father. If we are called to be imitators of Christ, we want to do things just as He did them. As you pray consistently each day, Jesus will set you up in love and unselfishness so as to walk right into what you are praying about, whether you pray seconds every day, minutes, or hours, but according to your walk with the Master, He will respond to you. In Hosea 6:6, it says, *For I delight in loyalty rather than sacrifice, and in the knowledge of God rather than burnt offerings.* Our God loves our loyalty to Him. Let's not strain at this concept of obedience and loyalty is better than sacrifice. Sacrifice is not at all like the other two, so we are not comparing apples to apples, so to speak. It would be like apples to an orange. Jesus is not saying sacrifice is bad—not at all. He is saying that obedience and loyalty is better, and He would rather have the two than the sacrifice. After all, if you ask yourself, "What good is a sacrifice made if you do not obey Jesus or you have no loyalty (relationship) with Him?"

How do we do things Jesus' way? If we were to read Ephesians 4:22–32, we would get a real good idea. The word is asking us to lay aside the old self and to put on a new self. What the difference would be is as individual as each person is, but what is consistent is how the new man would be in Christ. We are to start renewing our minds with His righteousness and holiness of truth. We are not to lie anymore, but we are to speak truth. If there is anger, be careful with it and do not let the sun go down without dealing with it in a proper way. We are not to steal anymore, but we are to work an honest job. Our speech should be clean, and not slanderous, but edifying to others. We are to be kind, tenderhearted, and forgiving one to another. We as Christians are not to grieve the Holy Spirit, by causing grief, sorrow, or offense. As we go about practicing these things, our relationship with Jesus grows, and so does the fragrance we carry of Him.

Jesus loved fragrances. We can tell this by the conversation in John 12. Mary, Lazarus's sister, poured pure nard on Jesus' feet and wiped them with her hair. He made reference that the remainder would be used for His burial. In Luke 7:37, we have an immoral woman who did a similar thing to Jesus' feet. She broke an alabaster vial full of perfume on His feet, and with tears of repentance, it says she continually kissed and wiped His feet with her hair. In those days, feet were very disgusting with dirt and dung from animals on them. It is clear by verse 44 that Jesus' feet were not washed when He came into Simon's house, so she was kissing perhaps very dirty feet.

As you have read this chapter and understand the question of what you smell like and how do you think you smell, are you well on your way to smelling great to the King? Have you a fragrance on you that cause Him to want more, a sweet smell? We know that He knows His children, but do His children know Him? We must cause a relationship. We must communicate with the Master as to what His plan is. We must be generous givers to further the kingdom and the causes Jesus creates within His plans for us. From Genesis 4, where Abel's offering of his best was accepted and Cain's offering was not, to Revelations 8:4, where the incense of the prayers of the saints are talked about, it is clear that Jesus loves fragrances. As the remainder of this book unfolds certain ways of bringing you closer to the Master, you still have to implement them. Just reading them won't do it. As it says in James 1:22, *but prove yourselves doers of the word, and not merely hearers who delude themselves.*

Now I know that my words here are meaningless, but I have given enough scripture for you to go out and practice and not to be hearers only and delude yourself. To delude ones' self would be to mislead your belief system, and to try and bring half truths which are nothing more than total lies to what scripture is instructing us to do.

You remember Psalm 23:5a, where it says, *You prepare a table before me in the presence of my enemies.* While this is true, you still have to pull yourself up to the table to enjoy and partake of what He has prepared. So how about it? Are you ready to further your walk with the King? Are you encouraged to spend a little more time with Jesus? If you are remembering nothing at this point, try to remember this, you can ask Him anything, and I mean anything. What ever it is you ask Him in your private moments, follow your question with "What do you think?" Believe me, Jesus will answer you. When you ask Him what He thinks, He is compelled to answer. As flesh, blood, and bone, we carry disgusting sins, and the Master knows each one of them. Where we will do well is to talk these over with Him in our secret places. Ask Him what you should do with them. You must believe He has your best interests in mind at all times and that He desires His will for you. When you give Him the chance to correct your sins, you will be set free with a true freedom, one that brings peace and true love to the equation. I cannot at this time stress the point enough when I say, " you must tell Him everything" leave out no detail.

Our God, Jesus, the Living Son of God, knows how you smell.

CHAPTER 9

Changing Your Harvest

*Do not be deceived, God is not mocked; for whatever a man
sows, this he will also reap. For the one who sows to his own
flesh will from the flesh reap corruption, but the one who sows
to the Spirit will from the Spirit reap eternal life.*—Galatians
6:7–8

We know for a fact that everyone has the ability to change their harvests
and the frequency of receiving our harvests. I am sure you just don't want
one harvest and that's it. I would like to look at several happenings in the Bible and
see if they changed their harvests or not. Are you ready? I know I am.

We know that one of the greatest happenings in the Bible about turning what
was given you into something great would be Joseph. In Genesis chapters 39 to 41,
it tells how Joseph was sold by the Ishmaelites to Potiphar, an Egyptian officer. It
says that all Joseph did was a success because the Lord was with him. Joseph did so
well that Potiphar made him his personal servant and put everything in Joseph's
charge. It says that the Lord blessed Potiphar because of Joseph. This is what today's
Christian should desire. We should want that whomever we work for should be
blessed because of us, because we have God's favor.

Trouble came to Joseph when Potiphar's wife wanted to sleep with him. She
desired him. What did Joseph do to change his harvest? You are right if you guessed
that he ran. Argument could be raised here as to changing his harvest. As it stands,
the world would probably say, "Sleep with her" because no one would find out and
things would be status quo. However, Joseph opted to run, and run he did. He

ran so fast he left his coat, and that is what did him in. With his garment in her hand, she screamed that he approached her with wrong motives, and he ended up in prison. Somehow this does not look like a change in harvest for the better. The word tells us that the Lord was with Joseph in prison. We need to know that when we walk through the valley of the shadow of death, He is with us every time.

We see that as Joseph was serving his time in prison for a crime he did not commit, he is again shown favor by the Lord. The jailer sees that Joseph is blessed and puts him in charge. Joseph, whether you realize it or not, is in the process of changing his harvest. He could be angry, bitter, and have an attitude of nonconformance, but he chooses to work hard where his feet are and the Lord was blessing it. I want you to be aware of a truth here. The Lord at times will put us in harm's way, but rest assured that He is right there with us all the way. We have a cupbearer and a baker coming into play here, and even though Joseph interprets their dreams, he gets no immediate help from them. As a matter of fact, he is forgotten about for two more years. Now, not all of us are put in this kind of situation, but big trials bring big victories. When you sow seeds of peace as Joseph was doing, the Lord changes the harvest to reap righteousness. Psalms 126:5 says, *Those who sow in tears shall reap with joyful shouting.* The word does not say, but I do believe Joseph shed some tears while in prison, but they did not over take his willingness to serve, which is what put him eventually over the top.

You never know whom you are with at times in your life, and Joseph and the chief cupbearer are no exception. As I said earlier, it was two full yeas later that Pharaoh had a dream, and Joseph was finally remembered. He was liberated from the dungeon and cleaned up to go before Pharaoh. It did not take Pharaoh long to figure out that Joseph not only interpreted his dream correctly but that he was the right man for the job to carry it out. We soon find that Joseph was second in the land only when Pharaoh sat on the throne; otherwise, Joseph was number one in Egypt. What a mighty blessing. Big trials reap big rewards. Big sowing reaps big harvests. Joseph went on to save his entire family. He willingly changed his harvest with great work ethics and a willingness to serve at all cost. Seeds sown must come to maturity for the harvest to be at its best, and only Jesus knows when you should reap it, which is just another reason you need Him daily. Remember that no one can cheat you out of what God has planned for you , but you yourself. You must realize that God has got your back, which will result in a much better future.

Ruth

We find in the book of Ruth that she stays with her mother-in-law and looks after her while the other daughter-in-law went back to her people. This action on the part of Ruth is in fact her change of harvest. In Ruth 2:10–12 it says, *Then she fell on her face, bowing to the ground and said to him, "Why have I found favor in your sight that you should take notice of me, since I am a foreigner?" Boaz replied to her, "All that you have done for your mother-in-law after the death of your husband has been fully reported to me, and how you left your father and your mother and the land of your birth and came to a people that you did not previously know. May the Lord reward your work and your wages be full from the Lord, the God of Israel, under whose wings you have come to seek refuge."* Ruth was a woman of humility and a hard worker. It is clear in chapter 2 that Boaz, the owner of the field, was granting her favor. This favor was from the Lord through Boaz. In Ruth 3:11, it tells us that *Ruth was a woman of excellence, and everyone in the city knew it.* Ladies, be women of excellence. One must work hard and be honest to achieve excellence in an entire city. Ruth was changing her harvest, and it was a big one. Ruth married Boaz, a wealthy landowner, and the lineage of David started with Boaz and Ruth, which was then traced to Jesus. If you go one generation back, you find that Boaz's mother was Rahab. Ruth 4:17 says, *The neighbor women gave him a name, saying, "A son has been born to Naomi!" So they named him Obed. He is the father of Jesse, the father of David.*

This was truly a game-changer for Ruth, a massive harvest change because of faithfulness, humility, and a willingness to serve, which was a small price to pay for such a change in harvest. Had she gone to be with her people when Naomi first wanted to release her of her family duties, she would have missed out on an enormous blessing and lineage right. When we are in daily prayer with the Lord we do not miss these opportunities because He is the one who sets you up to receive them as a change in harvests.

Esther

In the book of Esther, we find that a decree went out to find a replacement for Vashti, the queen. She was being replaced for not obeying the king's command. She had embarrassed the king and all his princes, so Vashti would be exiled. Now Mordecai was raising Hadassah, who was Esther, as she had no mother or father. We find that Esther was given great favor with Hegai, who was in charge of the women. Esther 2:9 says, *Now the young lady pleased him and found favor with him. So he quickly provided her with her cosmetics and food, gave her seven choice maids from the king's palace, and transferred her and her maids to the best place in the harem.* We will find that Esther is about to start to change her harvest. As was the custom, whoever went into the king's chamber could bring any type of jewelry or body adornment that pleased them. When it was Esther's turn, she asked the eunuch Hegai what the king liked. She went to the king's chamber, and the king liked her best over all of them, and he made her queen. Yes, she was beautiful, and she went through the rituals of beautification as follows: six months with oil of myrrh, six months with spices, and the cosmetics for women, but she was a servant, and went in to the king with apparel and jewelry that the king liked. It seems here that a little servant hood went a long way in changing Esther's harvest for the better, to say the least.

As time goes on, Mordecai hears of a plot to kill the king, and with Esther's help, they save the king. Mordecai was never rewarded for this, but the seed of a job well done is planted, and the harvest will come soon enough. I would like to further say that this is a perfect example of what we all run into from time to time, a job well done but no thank-you. We can take offense by this and ruin our blessings because the enemy was given room to steal it, or we can believe that Jesus has our backs and best interests in mind, and our deeds will not go unnoticed by Him (Hebrews 4:13).

We learn of a man here named Haman, who is not a good man, and he does not have a servant's heart—only to himself. He plots against the Jews to get rid of them all, but he will be stopped by Esther and Mordecai because they are willing to change their harvests. We find in Chapter 3 that Haman wants to rid the country of the Jews, and so tells the king it would be in his best interest to do so by a letter sealed with the king's signet ring that all Jews be annihilated. Now Mordecai and Esther are in anguish about this letter sent out to all the provinces to kill the Jews. Esther realizes through Mordecai that her royalty perhaps was in design by the Living God to save the Jews in such a time as this. Esther now plans to change her harvest again. Esther is a queen now and could turn her head, and ignore the problem and who would be the wiser, but she decides to put herself on the line again to change her harvest forever.

In Esther4:16, it says, *Go, assemble all the Jews who are found in Susa, and fast for me; do not eat or drink for three days, night or day. I and my maidens also will fast in the same way. And thus I will go in to the king, which is not according to the law, and if I perish, I perish.* The queen called a fast to seek the Lord's favor that would allow Esther to enter the king's court unannounced, which by custom, if the king's scepter is not raised, she will die right there. A true game-changer, a huge harvest change was about to come because she was planting seeds of servant hood that could take her life if not given the Lord's favor when she enters the king's court. Esther's plot was to expose Haman as the bad guy against the Jews, and she succeeded triumphantly. Haman plotted and built a gallows to hang Mordecai on it, but it backfired and Haman was made to honor Mordecai in the streets publicly. Haman was exposed, he and his entire family were put to death, Mordecai was exalted in the kingdom, and Esther went on to remain the queen. Our God is so good!

The riches and the protection that the change of harvest brought was enormous. Had Mordecai and Esther not stood up as Jews to defend their people, the outcome would have been drastically different. They both could have kept quiet and let the rest die, but they chose to put their lives on the line, which the Bible calls true love. How many of us have kept quiet in matters we could have spoken up on? How many times have we turned a blind eye and a deaf ear to things we should have stuck up for or did something about? If we are faithful in the small things, we will then be faithful in the bigger things of life. If you want to be like Esther or Mordecai, and you can, you must start out with the small issues of life and stand up for the scriptures with your families and friends.

Pastors, you have to stop compromising the gospel for the sake of the tithe. John 15:13 says, *Greater love has no one than this, that one lay down his life for his friends.* This verse is attainable, but we must first stand up for our beliefs with those around us, including our own children.

Deborah

Now Deborah, a prophetess, the wife of Lappidoth, was judging Israel at that time. She used to sit under the palm tree of Deborah between Ramah and Bethel in the hill country of Ephraim, and the sons of Israel came up to her for judgment (Judges 4:4–5).

What a legacy to have as a child of the Living God, to have written that you are a prophetess, a wife, a judge of Israel, a warrior, and a singer of her own song. She would sit under the palm tree of Deborah, and the people would come to her for judgment. It was here that the Lord set her up for victory. She sent for Barak the commander of the army of Israel and prophesied that he would defeat the oppressive army of the Canaanites. Now Barak was not feeling so valiant when she spoke this over him. As a matter of fact, he said that he would not go unless she went with him. It says in Judges 4:8, ***Then Barak said to her, "If you will go with me, then I will go; but if you will not go with me, I will not go."***

This spoken word from Barak says a mouthful about Deborah. I believe he thought of her as a woman of both strong mind and of good physical fitness. Had Barak had any reservations of fighting the opposing army, he would not have added to his worry with a woman that was weak in mind and body. However, Barak changed his harvest from greatness in conquering the enemy alone to a shared victory with Deborah. Barak's faith was not that of Deborah's faith. On the other hand, at this point Deborah changed her harvest from prophetess to victorious warrior. She sowed seeds of the word of the Living God and believed in them to a point of putting her life on the line with her faith in complete action.

In Matthew 17:20 it says, ***And He said to them, "Because of the littleness of your faith; for truly I say to you, if you have faith the size of a mustard seed, you will say to this mountain, Move from here to there, and it will move, and nothing will be impossible to you."*** I believe right here Deborah exercised this scripture in her time. She believed in what the Lord told her to tell Barak to the point of going to war. What the Lord said to her, she believed with her life. Barak, on the other hand, reduced his harvest by not trusting God's word for him. Remember the Lord intended the victory for Barak only.

"Wives, be subject to your own husbands, as to the Lord. For the husband is the head of the wife, as Christ also is the head of the church, He Himself being the Savior of the body" (Ephesians 5:22–23). Also, "Therefore humble yourselves under the mighty hand of God, that He may exalt you at the proper time" (1 Peter 5:6). Even though these scriptures came after Deborah's time I believe we can look back and see that she fulfilled these in their entirety. How do I know this? Because the Lord called her" a mother in Israel," and His favor was upon her to change her harvest to one of complete greatness. She was a virtuous woman (Proverbs 31:10).

As Deborah prophesied over Barak, and he declined unless she come with him, she with great humility reminded him that victory would not be his alone but also given to a woman. When we serve with humility and respect the authority over us, the Lord will exalt us in due time. When you think about the greatness of Deborah and what the Lord allowed her to accomplish, she was a woman with a sword in her hand and a song in her heart while judging Israel and managing her family. A multi-tasked person of her day.

If you feel like you want to change your harvest, maybe you want to take a closer look at Deborah and know Jesus wants this harvest for you too. You do not have to lead ten thousand men into battle to be God's warrior, and you do not have to judge a nation to be heard among men and women. Jesus wants you to be victorious, and He wants you walking into your prayers. The Lord will always set you up, so as you pray, listen! Jesus will begin to feed you things to pray for that might not make sense to you at the moment. When this happens, I suggest you journal them with dates so you will know how far out the Lord has you in prayer, so as to walk into them in the future. These are faith builders!

I believe that everyone understands the concept of seed sowing to get a harvest. One seed when planted will produce a plant with multiplied seeds on it. You can save half for future seed plantings for more harvests and you can eat half and enjoy the fruits of your labors. There are several more scriptures pertaining to sowing and harvesting, and this chapter is not meant to be a definitive compilation of every one. I hope I have given you something to think about and pursue in Christ Jesus.

All of us, whether reading this book or not, are faced with decisions that will change our harvests. Harvests require seed, and seed can be money given to a cause, a time investment, or a decision of faith, etc. When we make these decisions, they alter our lives. With this in mind, you and I want to know how and when to make these decisions count, and the only way this can happen on a regular basis is to stay in communication with the one who makes them happen. Jesus is the answer, pure and simple. The eternal question is whether you will ask of Him the answer.

As the very first scripture I gave in this chapter (Galatians 6:7–8) states, "Do not be deceived, God is not mocked; for whatever a man sows, this he will also reap." We do not fool Jesus. Hebrews 4:13 says, *And there is no creature hidden from His sight, but all things are open and laid bare to the eyes of Him with whom we have to do.* The Word really tells us how easy it can be. We just need to ask of the One who makes it all happen. Whether seven seconds or seven minutes with Him, you will get your answer. Time spent with the Master does parallel the severity of the task set before us. Consistency with Him is the answer. My prayer for you as you finish reading these last few words in this chapter is that your relationship with Jesus has grown since chapter one and that you are already seeing answers to your questions from time spent with the Master. It is good to hear the word of God, but it is better to be doers of the word so we won't delude ourselves (James 1:22). Now go…and practice.

Before we go to the next chapter lets look at one of the many true happenings to change our harvest in our church when we were feeding the homeless and those less fortunate. There were several times that we were faced with empty cupboards and nothing for the following week as we would feed the homeless every Saturday from noon to 1 o'clock pm. Never ever did we fall short. Never did we turn anyone away, we always had food for the day. Like it says in Matthew 14: 17-20 … *and He said, Bring them here to Me". Ordering the people to sit down on the grass, He took the five loaves and the two fish, and looking up toward heaven, He blessed the food, and breaking the loaves He gave them to the disciples, and the disciples gave them to the crowds, and they all ate and were satisfied.*

This particular happening unfolded like this; it was a typical Saturday where we fed several people and there was no food left. We had fed the last person and as he was sitting there enjoying the meal we had provided for him, Carole who was in charge of this ministry said to me, "pastor we have nothing left, only this package of cheese and crackers" and the gentleman sitting there eating his meal yelled, "I'll take it" we laughed and of course gave it to him. The Lord took us down to the last cracker and had us give that away. Carole said to me, " what are we going to do, there is nothing left for next week?". I told her it was not our problem, but only the Lords' because He told me, " if you pray for my kingdom, I will take care of the stuff". So I told her not to worry, but to pray for a ministry in the church or some-one she knew and we would see what the Lord has planned. The Lord loves to create situations where out of nothing comes something... Him! The following Monday I received a call from my son-in-law Ryan that his boss felt compelled to give to a mission somewhere and did he know of anyone or place that he could give to? Ryan told him about us and he wrote out a check for $1,000.00. Is God not faithful? Is He not good? We must be willing to be put into these positions of want, need, and lack in order to see His work be done. Needless to say my wife and I called Carole and said, "lets go shopping". You must be a willing vessel for the Lord to work this way, just be willing and pray, as He will do the rest. As an old friend once said," we are to do what we can, and He will do what we cannot".

We can change our harvests from average to good, from good to great, and from great to unbelievable, it just depends on what you will allow the Lord to do in your life. What ever you decide, just don't let the enemy steal your harvest.

CHAPTER 10

Crossing Over

Crossing over is making a conscientious decision to follow Christ in a manner that produces an action glorifying His kingdom and power, regardless of the circumstances.

First Crossing Over (Moses)

Then Moses stretched out his hand over the sea, and the Lord swept the sea back *by a strong east wind all night and turned the sea into dry land, so the waters were divided. The sons of Israel went through the midst of the sea on the dry land, and the waters* were like *a wall to them on their right hand and on their left* (Exodus 14:21–22).

This is crossing over from bondage to freedom. To the Israelites, this was the way the Lord provided for them to escape slavery by the Egyptians. Can you imagine the walls of water as they passed through to the other side? Who knows really how high the walls of water were. One thing we do know for sure is they passed through on dry ground. They didn't have to travel in the muck and soupy mud. The Lord made travel easy over dry ground. Our God thinks of everything.

The Israelites literally crossed over the Red Sea from bondage to freedom. We as Christians must cross over metaphorically. We are bound to the world, enslaved to what it has to offer us, and we must allow the Lord to cross us over into freedom, a true freedom, in Jesus. When we look at this passage, we can see the power of the Living God at work. In each of our lives, we have bondages or fears that keep us from being and achieving who we are and what we are called to do. The east winds are the powers of the Living God called out by Him to drive back the forces that keep us from our destinies. As the deep sea kept the Israelites from their freedom, so the sea metaphorically keeps us from our freedom. The sea in life is all of life that holds us back. I for one want the Lord to use His east wind to drive back that which holds me back, don't you? I want my Lord to create a passage for me so I can cross over to freedom, a place of liberty, and I would like it on dry ground too.

Now the Lord is the Spirit, and where the Spirit of the Lord is, there *is liberty* (2 Corinthians 3:17).

When we hear about God's liberty, we also can know that the chains of life will fall off and be broken. These chains are things and issues of life that hold you and weigh you down. Chains can be people, things, and words wrongly spoken or wrongly taken in offense, etc. Whatever is master over you is what will chain you down. Whatever is holding you back from going forward in Christ is a chain. Our God loosens the chains to the point that they fall off.

> *When you pray for the Lord to break the chains that bind you, there will be such a violent pull by the enemy just before they break... you will make it, He will see to it that you do.*

And suddenly there came a great earthquake, so that the foundations of the prison house were shaken, and immediately all the doors were opened and everyone's chains were unfastened (Acts 16:26). This is the God I serve. He breaks every chain so we can cross over to freedom. I don't want to give you a false impression that when you cross over, every situation for you will be great. I believe there was fear in the eyes of the Israelites passing over the Red Sea. The walls of water could have been intimidating to say the least. Maybe they thought that these walls of water could come crashing down any time. We know two things for sure. One, the walls didn't come down on them. The walls of water were saved for the enemy—in their case, the Egyptians. The second thing we know is every one of the Israelites made it to the other side to freedom.

I believe as I write this book that this crossing over is prophetic for many of you as you read it and believe that the Lord wants you to cross over so you can partake of the special things He has designed just for you. I believe that many of you have been mistreated at your workplace and have kept a godly attitude. You are about to cross over to that promotion and pay raise. I also believe with great conviction that many of you have been held back. You have been kept from advancing forward in life due to finances, sickness, and family. Perhaps you have been degraded in some way by people that have caused you to be held up, to be in a form of bondage. Let the Lord use His east wind and set you free. You have perhaps been spoken over in prophecy that you were to relocate, but it seems to have never taken place. Well, hold on, your east wind is coming to set you on your course to freedom, to relocate. I believe that the Lord has a spiritual liberty just for you. Why would I say such things when I don't even know you. It is first and foremost not about me or what I say, but it is about His word, and that word is for you. So claim it with everything you have.

Do you need to cross over in your walk with Jesus? Do you need a better marriage? Do you want ministry or the one you are in to grow? Do you need greater finances? Let the Lord cross you over. Let His east wind form walls from what the enemy has laid before you as obstructions for so many years. The walls formed by the enemy's obstructions in your life are testimonies of God's greatness, but in order to experience this, we must be willing to walk through them.

I want to take a minute and address the pastors who are reading this book. A reminder here that the grumbling of the people was constant. Do not give up. Get on your face to the Living God on behalf of your flock. Jesus will get you through! Know that the Living God wants you to cross over from bondage to freedom as well. Pastors can acquire chains and bondages as well, so let the Lord free you! Your prayers should cry out for your flock yes, but your flock needs to cry out for the community, then you will all cross over.

Second Crossing Over (Joshua)

It shall come about when the soles of the feet of the priests who carry the ark of the Lord, the Lord of all the earth, rest in the waters of the Jordan, the waters of the Jordan will be cut off, and the waters which are flowing down from above will stand in one heap...And the priests who carried the ark of the covenant of the Lord stood firm on dry ground in the middle of the Jordan while all Israel crossed on dry ground, until the entire nation had finished crossing the Jordan (Josh. 3:13–17).

This is a different crossing over from the Red Sea. This crossing over was at the Jordan River when the water was at its highest during harvest season (verse 15). As believers in Christ, we want to welcome both crossings. If you are reading this book and have not accepted Jesus as your Lord and savior and you have made it this far, I believe you are ready. Accept Him as your savior and let Him cross you over. To believe in Jesus as your savior, you need to embrace John 1:1–4, *"In the beginning was the Word, and the Word was with God, and the Word was God. He was in the beginning with God. All things came into being through Him, and apart from Him nothing came into being that has come into being. In Him was life, and the life was the Light of men."*

You need to embrace the cross, as He died for you and me, that our sins be forgiven us through His death and resurrection. *All Scripture is inspired by God and profitable for teaching, for reproof, for correction, for training in righteousness, so that the man of God may be adequate, equipped for every good work* (2 Timothy 3:16–17). And we must believe all the scriptures, not what we pick and choose.

This particular crossing over is one of crossing from wilderness or a wandering to a place of inheritance. We as people without Christ are wanderers. He is a God with a plan. As we have talked periodically throughout this book, it is wise to get His directions to His plan for each of us. In order for this to take place, we must have communication. When we exercise this prayer time and communication, the Lord can guide us across our Jordan River.

Here, the Lord did not permit the waters to separate until the soles of their feet touched the water. There is much to learn here. The Lord sometimes calls for faith right up to the last second before deliverance of a situation. The soles of their feet had to touch the water, and it was the priest's soles. Here we need to understand that there is a reason the Lord used the priest's feet. They were the ones of Levitical heritage and were the only ones able to touch the Ark. We need to have pastoral guidance. Sometimes we need the faith of those who are called to the ministry to get us through. Those of us who are called to be pastors are called and equipped. When we as pastors have the relationship with Jesus that we should have, we will be willing to touch an overflowing Jordan with the soles of our feet and get those standing behind us to their inheritance.

We want to remember that this crossing over is one from wandering to inheritance. The wandering is a dangerous and most often nonproductive time in our walk with Jesus. This time of wandering has a harvest, believe it or not. It is a harvest of stagnancy. *Do not be deceived, God is not mocked; for whatever a man sows, this he will also reap. For the one who sows to his own flesh will from the flesh reap corruption, but the one who sows to the Spirit will from the Spirit reap eternal life. Let us not lose heart in doing good, for in due time we will reap if we do not grow weary* (Galatians 6:7 9). When we wander, it is aimless and usually in circles. It keeps us from moving forward with Christ. Jesus loves us unconditionally wherever we are in life, but He does not want us to stay there. When we wander, we usually are faced with situations of life that we do not want to deal with. They will not go away by themselves. Maybe you are facing addictions. There are the usual addictions of drinking, drugs, and smoking, but what about addiction to you? When we put ourselves first, we lose our first love, Jesus. He is always with us no matter what, but we just can't hear or see Him in what we are doing. How about your church? Are you as a congregation wandering? Does it seem that you are in stagnation? Jesus wants you to cross over to your inheritance. He has no doubt given you a vision or has prophesied a direction, then seek Him as to why the waters have not parted.

Joshua was crossing the people over from wandering to the promise. What have you been promised? God's promises are true: *"But now take courage, Zerubbabel," declares the LORD, "take courage also, Joshua son of Jehozadak, the high priest, and all you people of the land take courage," declares the LORD, "and work, for I am with you," declares the LORD of hosts. "As for the promise which I made you when you came out of Egypt, My Spirit is abiding in your midst; do not fear!"* (Haggai 2:4–5). Here the Lord is reassuring His people that He has not left them since they left Egypt. Our Lord will not leave us either, and we must not fear. Remember the Lord is Shammah, the God who is there. He is already across to the other side waiting for your foot steps. Go ahead and ask Him what it will take to part the waters.

Make sure that *your character is free from the love of money, being content with what you have; for He Himself has said, "I will never desert you, nor will I ever forsake you, " so that we confidently say, "The Lord is my helper; I will not be afraid. What will man do to me?"* (Hebrews 13:5–6). The Lord will not abandon us, ever. As we are in our wandering, repetitious life, God's love is there. As we draw close to Him and bring Him in to our wandering, He then allows us to walk into our prayers. If we go back to the original scripture of the Israelites crossing the Jordan, it says, *It shall come about when the soles of the feet of the priests who carry the ark of the Lord, the Lord of all the earth, rest in the waters of the Jordan, the waters of the Jordan will be cut off,* and *the waters which are flowing down from above will stand in one heap.*

So when we decide to trust the Lord with our issues, He will cause the issues (waters of the Jordan) to stop and cause them to heap up or form a wall. This allows us then to walk through these issues on dry land. When we walk with Jesus in trust, He is there to see us through. ***For I am* confident of this very thing, that He who began a good work in you will perfect it until the day of Christ Jesus** (Philippians 1:6). Some people would say that we must just put our foot on the water in faith and it will part, but I do not think that is the issue here, nor was it for Peter. We must seek the Living God as to what will part the water when our shoe hits it, then the water will part. We must go with faith, and knowing His direction and timing will give us this faith. You must include Him in everything, and not go half baked with maybes and call it faith. That kind of going will cause nothing but heart ache and failure.

We must stand on His promises. His promises are like blank checks with His signature on them, and we can cash them in at any time. My God has an endless account. It does not matter how long it's been since you were promised something prophetically. What matters is that you pursue Him. Do not worry if you have seemingly been passed over in your job or even at your church. What you must do is pursue the one who blesses you, the one who is truly the provider. Now is the time to pursue Jireh the Lord, your provider, and allow Him to make good on His promises. Realign yourself with the Holy One, the King of kings, and the Lord of lords. Return to your first love and let Him cross you over from wandering to His promise for you. Your destiny and future are in your trusting Him. In John 10:10

it says, *The thief comes only to steal and kill and destroy; I came that they may have life, and have* it *abundantly.* Do not let the enemy steal from you anymore. Do not let the enemy kill your dreams and prophecies that have been spoken over you. Do not let the enemy destroy your destiny in Christ. Jesus says He came to bring life. So let Him breathe life into you right where you are. Let Him breathe abundant life into your steps.

I want to pray for you as you read this book. I have prayed for years about what the Lord would have me write. I can tell you this: my faith soars in Jesus' name for you. I believe you will have victories in Jesus' name. I believe for you, that if you lay your hand on your heart and close your eyes and breathe out the name Jesus, He will be right there for you. How do I know this? There are two scriptures that come to my mind that I can truly say I embrace fully for this matter. One is, *Now behold, today I am going the way of all the earth, and you know in all your hearts and in all your souls that not one word of all the good words which the Lord your God spoke concerning you has failed; for you all have been fulfilled, not one of them has failed* (Joshua 23:14).

Now I realize that my God is the only one who knows how many days I have left upon this earth, but I can truly say that the forty years I have been walking with Him, He has not forsaken me once. He has fulfilled everything and failed me in nothing. Second, in Psalms 37:25 it says, *I have been young and now I am old, yet I have not seen the righteous forsaken or his descendants begging bread.* Not once have I been forsaken by my God nor have I had to beg for bread in my days of walking with the Master, not once. There is something to say for age, and that is longevity of God's consistent care for His children. My forty years bears testimony to His faithful care to me and my wife.

Whether you are crossing over from bondage to freedom or you are crossing over from wandering to the promise, there is no power of the enemy strong enough to stop you unless you allow it. Pharaoh represents the enemy who wishes to enslave us to the standards of the world. The verses tell us that all Pharaoh's chariots and horses could not come against what the Living God had for His people, and I am here to tell you that it means the same for you too. Every form of darkness that comes against you will fail. *No weapon that is formed against you will prosper, and every tongue that accuses you in judgment you will condemn. This is the heritage of the servants of the Lord, and their vindication is from Me, declares the Lord* (Isaiah 54:17). The truth of this scripture is you staying close to the Lord. Stay in His righteousness and seek His Holiness.

Remember the enemy is the accuser of the brethren, and he will use every opportunity to point his finger in your direction if he can. *Then I heard a loud voice in Heaven, saying, "Now the salvation, and the power, and the kingdom of our God and the authority of His Christ have come, for the accuser of our brethren has been thrown down, he who accuses them before our God day and night"* (Revelations 12:10).

We never want to give the enemy grounds for finger pointing. He is playing for keeps with anything he can steal, kill, or destroy. The Lord said Himself that these are the only three things the enemy comes to do. A good litmus test would then be to ask is what is happening in your life right now that he is trying to steal from you? Is there confusion, is there a form of killing in your life, or are you seeing a destruction going on? If there is the slightest resemblance, then it is not of God, and you must get rid of it in Jesus' name. Prayer is the answer, and the statement to the Lord that you want and need His help is paramount here. Jesus only comes to bring life and life more abundantly. Prayer when done right in Gods' eyes is one of the most powerful weapons you could have against the forces of evil. You should want to use it.

Other Types of Crossing Over

But David went back and forth from Saul to tend his father's flock at Bethlehem (1 Samuel 17:15).

And David put his hand into his bag and took from it a stone and slung it *and struck the Philistine on his forehead. And the stone sank into his forehead, so that he fell on his face to the ground* (1 Samuel 17:49).

We see that for a long time, David, after he was anointed king by Samuel, went back and forth from the army camp to the sheep. A repetition of the same old, same old. One day David was faced with a decision of whether to confront Goliath or return to his father's sheep. David crossed over not when he ran to the battle line, but when he drew the stone from his bag and put it in his sling. When he drew his weapon, Goliath knew he had an opponent. David's commitment came when he drew his weapon of choice. We, like David, must make our choices as well. We must not only face our Goliaths but also draw our weapons of choice. In the Christian's case, it is prayer and the Word. Prayer moves mountains with faith, and the Word speaks it out.

Rahab

Then Joshua the son of Nun sent two men as spies secretly from Shittim, saying, Go view the land, especially Jericho. So they went and came into the house of a harlot whose name was Rahab and lodged there. And the king of Jericho sent word to Rahab, saying, Bring out the men who have come to you, who have entered your house, for they have come to search out all the land. But the woman had taken the two men and hidden them, and she said, Yes, the men came to me, but I did not know where they were from…Now therefore, please swear to me by the Lord, since I have dealt kindly with you, that you also will deal kindly with my father's household, and give me a pledge of truth, and spare my father and my mother and my brothers and my sisters, with all who belong to them, and deliver our lives from death. —Joshua 2:1, 3, 4, 12, 13

I believe Rahab was a woman of business, and she was successful at it. Her house was on the wall of Jericho, and she seized an opportunity for her and her family. I also believe Rahab crossed over when she was face-to-face with the spies. I believe that we as Christians must have answers to questions before we go out into the world. When we are faced with decisions, we must have the answers already established in our heart, or we will go with the flow of the world. This is where I believe praying daily helps us. By praying to the King on a daily basis, we hear the answers from Him, and so the same with Rahab. She had her mind made up because of what she had heard the God of the Israelites did when crossing the Red Sea. So when she saw the spies, she knew to take the opportunity and use it. Her faith was so great that she is mentioned with other Bible greats in the New Testament. This was her crossing over. Whether she was committing treason to her country or not, she knew which route to take, and the Lord saved her and her family.

What is so great about this is that Rahab was the mother of Boaz, who married Ruth...

Esther

For if you remain silent at this time, relief and deliverance will arise for the Jews from another place and you and your father's house will perish. And who knows whether you have not attained royalty for such a time as this? Then Esther told them to reply to Mordecai, Go, assemble all the Jews who are found in Susa, and fast for me; do not eat or drink for three days, night or day. I and my maidens also will fast in the same way. And thus I will go in to the king, which is not according to the law, and if I perish, I perish. So Mordecai went away and did just as Esther had commanded him.—(Esther 4:14–17)

Esther's moment of crossing over was when she heard the report through Hathach from Mordecai about Haman wanting to kill all the Jews. She could have hid behind the fact that she was queen. No one would have found out that she herself was a Jew. She decided to stick up for her people and acknowledge the one true God. She called a fast for everyone in Susa, herself, and her maidens. Sometimes the Lord requires us to step out and be counted among them. Sometimes we need to stand up for what we know is right even if it costs us our position at work or with family and friends. Esther put everything on the line in faith that the Lord would deliver them, and He did deliver them with blessings galore. Esther and Mordecai had high positions, just as many of you hold in this world. Do not think that the Lord overlooks this. Yes, you may be in danger of losing your position when sticking up for right, but know that Jesus is right there with you every step of the way. If you were to lose your position in standing up for Christ, know this, you are His child and He has a better one for you. Trust and obey, there is no other way.

Jesus

They were saying this, testing Him, so that they might have grounds for accusing Him. But Jesus stooped down and with His finger wrote on the ground. But when they persisted in asking Him, He straightened up, and said to them, "He who is without sin among you, let him be the first to throw a stone at her." Again He stooped down and wrote on the ground (John 8:6–8).

Jesus truly crossed over here. His faith is not in question, but His faith became action. Some men of the town conveniently found a woman who was in the act of sexual relations. They brought her out, but not the man, and threw her down in front of Jesus. He stooped and wrote in the sand. We don't know for sure what He was writing, but what came next is crucial to crossing over. They persisted in testing and asking Him what should be done with her. Jesus then stood up and said to them, "He who is without sin among you, let him be the first to throw a stone at her."

They all had stones in their hands and could have easily used them on Jesus as well as her. Jesus stood up for right. He stood up for the woman and protected her. We are faced with this almost daily. Our opponents might not have rocks in their hands, ready to throw them, but they do stand for an apposing view of the gospel. We either shrink back and say nothing or stand up as Jesus did and side with the gospel. Either way, the answer is tucked in our hearts before we leave the house— yes, our minds are made up before we are faced with the question. If we do not side with the gospel, the only other way is to side with the world, and that is to side with the devil and his cohorts.

If I could talk to the pastors for a moment that are reading this book. You and your spouse need to cross over well before your congregation. You are called to lead the sheep, it is your mantel to carry. You and your church need both types of crossing over, first to freedom, then to the promise. It is in the promises that your churches victories lie. The only way to claim Jeremiah 29:11 is to go through verses 7,8,9, and 10. Just like claiming your city you must cross them over to the promise.

Jesus was a servant to its highest form, and we are to follow His lead. Each Christian will be faced with crossing over to show faith. We as believers also need the crossing over from bondage of the world to freedom in Christ, and the second crossing over from wandering in our faith to the promise given us with faith. We should welcome these in our walk with the Living God. When we pray daily, the Lord will see to it that we do not miss our chances, because we will hear Him speak to us. Remember in John 10:10, He has come to bring life, and life more abundantly.

CHAPTER 11

Now What?

Always learning and never able to come to the knowledge of the truth.—2 Timothy 3:7

But prove yourselves doers of the word, and not merely hearers who delude themselves. For if anyone is a hearer of the word and not a doer, he is like a man who looks at his natural face in a mirror; for once he has looked at himself and gone away, he has immediately forgotten what kind of person he was.—James 1:22–24

As you read this chapter, you will find that I have given you a recap of what you read. It is imperative as Christians that we go out and practice the word. You don't have to practice what I have written, but you must practice the scriptures. I do believe I have backed up with scriptures what I firmly believe Jesus has given me to write for you. I know what I have written to be true, and my God has not failed me, ever. If you practice these principles given in these pages, your walk with the Lord can only grow in a positive way. Each chapter, I used Bible happenings to explain what the Lord wants out of us. As you read these last lines, I will be speaking more of what you should do rather than what the Bible greats have already done.

Stepping out in Faith?

Now faith is the assurance of things *hoped for, the conviction of things not seen* (Hebrews 11:1).

I prefer to say stepping out *with* faith rather than *in* faith simply because the word *with* denotes a sense of fellowship with the Lord already. We know that faith pleases God so this is the route the Christian wants to go. Not everything you see in front of you will promote faith. You might have to dig deep in your very soul to draw it up. What the Lord is looking for in His children is trust in His ability to deliver. We need to trust when the Lord promises us something that He will be good to make it happen. We are called to pray it through.

The written word was then, and it is now! It is just as powerful now as it was in their times. What is the difference? It is our faith system. Hang on to the Word, and do not let it go for anything. I have a saying that people around me hear all the time. "Hang onto the hem of His garment, and do not let go." Jesus is looking for His children to endure and hang on to the very end.

Jesus walked on water, and so did Peter. I used to have a hard time believing this when I was young in the Lord because I could not (and still can't) walk on water. What I have learned from this happening between Peter and Jesus was what was said was more important than what was done. Jesus was walking on the water, and we don't generally have a problem with His ability to do that. However, Peter asked a question. He said to the Lord that if it was truly Him that Jesus would command him to come, and that is exactly what Jesus did. He said, "Come." This is so vital to remember in the scriptures. When you communicate in prayer with Jesus, you must believe He will answer you. Write down what you say, because He will respond to you. Don't let the winds of life scare you. It is the enemy coming to steal your blessing and nothing more.

In Mark 9:21–24, it says, *And He asked his father, "How long has this been happening to him?" And he said, "From childhood. It has often thrown him both into the fire and into the water to destroy him. But if You can do anything, take pity on us and help us!" And Jesus said to him, "If You can? All things are possible to him who believes." Immediately the boy's father cried out and said, "I do believe; help my unbelief!"*

Here is an example of what many of us feel at some point in our lives about the miracle powers of Jesus Christ. This man had a son who was possessed with a devil that made him mute and would throw him often in the fire or water to kill him. Jesus tells us in John 10:10 that the enemy only comes to steal, kill, and destroy… well, here is a classic example of it. I want to point out what the father said to Jesus in his initial talk about what he wanted for his son. The father said to Jesus, "If You can do anything, take pity on us and help us!"

This is where many of us are when we first encounter Christ and His miracle working love for us. We are in the "IF" stage. I think Jesus was a little taken aback by his comment of "IF." Jesus just found out his twelve disciples couldn't do anything, and now the word *if* comes out of the father's mouth. Remember, Jesus can handle our unbelief; we just can't stay in that realm. Jesus answers the man by saying, "'If You can?' All things are possible to him who believes." Remember that we must try to walk "with" faith in Jesus, but if we cry out the word "if," then be honest as the father of the boy was. Many of us at times are right here in this same situation. Our belief system is not strong enough so we must be honest with the Lord. He said, "I do believe; help my unbelief." Keep going, keep going, keep going—Jesus is with us all the way. His goal for us is to walk with faith.

Remember David as he faced Goliath. He reminded Goliath that the reason he was going to be defeated was because of what the Lord did for David in the past. David said that He had killed a lion and the bear for him and that Goliath going down today would be just like those. This is a truth to take to the bank—God's bank. When the Lord does something for you, bring it with you. Bring what God has done to the present, and by doing so with faith, you are allowing Jesus to create a better future for you. This is how you "walk with faith." Bring what God has already done for you in the past and apply it when speaking against the enemy in Jesus' name. Remind the enemy what Jesus has done and will do again.

Prayer

You have learned that prayer time with Jesus is as individual as your DNA is to anyone else. Whether you stand up, sit down, pace, or lie flat on the ground, facedown, you are as unique as you want to be in prayer.

When you pray you might need a fleece. Remember to write down what you ask the Lord. So often we don't, and when the Lord answers us according to our fleece, we get confused because we wrote nothing down, and now we are not sure as to what we asked. Sound familiar? If you do ask for a fleece, it should be fitting to the task at hand. Gideon was called to fight with an army whittled down from thousands to a mere three hundred to fight an army of more than one hundred and twenty thousand. He was afraid and needed to know God was in this and that it was not some notion of his own rattling between his ears. The important thing in a fleece is to write it down. Don't worry; the Lord isn't going to be looking for a loophole to escape. We are the ones who need the documentation. Gideon spent appropriate time with the Lord to find out directions and the plan of action. We need to heed this example and spend time with the Lord because He knows the plan.

Let's not walk away from this book still making prayer difficult. Prayer always was easy, and it still is. If you can talk to your friend, then you can talk to the Lord. Sorry—no ifs, ands, or buts about it. Talking comes natural to all of us. Jesus knows everything, but we need to speak it out to Him and journal it. When we journal, it will increase our faith by the mile.

WHEN JESUS IS BROUGHT INTO YOUR EQUATION OF LIFE IN SUCH A WAY AS TO DO NOTHING WITHOUT HIS CONSENT, YOU WILL REALIZE THERE IS NO SUCH THING AS "STEPPING OUT IN FAITH," but " STEPPING OUT WITH FAITH."

It might be difficult at first to journal, but when you get into the habit, your faith will soar like the eagle.

What He knows, I must know. What I know, He must know. I am compelled to tell Him, and he is compelled to listen. It is the way He wants it, a two-way street.

Jesus wants nothing more than a relationship with you. Your prayer life will cause this relationship to either go south or up, up, and up. Prayer to Him is not about reciting repetitious words over and over but a heartfelt communication of love between you and Jesus. This is why it is so unique. Talk to Him now, today. Don't wait another second, and when you do, tell Him everything.

Ask. Seek. Knock.

To use this acronym is to want to see a progression in your relationship with Jesus. This denotes pure action on our part in exercising our faith in the one true God. Asking the Lord something in prayer can be quite stationary but to seek Him takes action. This entire book is to help you seek Him. It is where your relationship lies with the creator. The knock will come automatically. When we have written down what we ask of Him, and we truly set out to seek the one who holds the answers, we can only believe that it is just a matter of His timing that we will in fact be ushered to the door of opportunity and knock on it.

Be careful here. Pride is the lock you put on your door of opportunity. Don't let pride get in your way here. Seek Him in such a way as to let humility walk with you.

The knock is just a formality. It is done only so the Lord can eagerly open the door for you. The door is presented to us when the seeking meets a requirement in our relationship with He who makes it all happen. As each asking is different from the previous, so likewise is the seeking different as we move closer and closer to the Lord. His requirements in us and for us change as we grow in Him. The doors change with the asking, and the opening of them gets greater and greater with each passing day with the Master.

As with the Syrophoenician woman, we need to exercise humility when asking and seeking the Lord in a matter. We must not let offense come and steal our blessing. The enemy does not want you to have anything from the Lord, so when he steals, he means it for keeps. Can you see yourself as a person who Jesus says that to help you it would be like giving bread for the Jews to dogs? Do you consider yourself a dog? She did not let it slow her down, though. What she asked for was far more important than some humbling comments. We have got to fight the enemy in love, and the love of Christ keeps us from offense.

As we pursue the Living God, we need to draw near to Him, and for us that means to be transparent with the creator that knows everything about us. We need to get close to the one who knows. We need to trust in Him and know that we can tell Him anything—that's right, anything. We need to understand that He understands the good, the bad, and the ugly of who we are. We must remember that without faith it is impossible to please Him. So in order to please Him, we must exercise what faith we have, and we have all been given a measure of it.

For through the grace given to me, I say to everyone among you not to think more highly of himself than he ought to think, but to think so as to have sound judgment, as God has allotted to each a measure of faith (Romans 12:3).

The easiest way to receive more faith is to tell Jesus everything, and I mean everything. Spill-your-guts type prayer. We need to get it off our chests so we can breathe in Christ freely so as to receive more of Him. Try it—you will like it, guaranteed!

Seven Seconds with God

Our God's yoke is easy, and His burden is light. There is nothing hard about our Living God. Bottom line with our Lord is this: we need relationship. What better way to start than seven seconds with Him? (Good morning, Lord! What can I do for your kingdom today? Will You please come with me today?) You are well on your way to creating a great time with the Master. We are the ones who draw a line in front of us and say, "This far, Lord, and no farther today. Sorry." We need to get rid of that line as best we can. Jesus does not wish to bring confusion to us. That type of thing is only from the enemy. He does not bring a fear to us either but a sound mind.

When you put it together, He wants to talk to us and tell us things. He will not make it difficult to do so. He is the one who has plans for us and wants us to know every one of them. You want to understand also at this point that you can cause your own confusion. When the enemy sees your state of mind, he just capitalizes on what you started. One way to stop this is to journal your prayers with the Lord. Many times our confusion is because we cannot quite remember what we prayed for and what we asked the Lord for in a fleece. You must listen to me here, and trust me, you will eliminate a lot of frustration just by journaling. You don't need to spend a lot of time journaling, but make sure you highlight the areas you want to remember. Spending time with the Lord, whether a short time or a long time, is important. I want to hear how you have grown with the Lord, and time spent with the Master is needed. Those who have a weak prayer time with Jesus have to start somewhere, and asking these three things will help you on a road to victory.

One piece of knowledge we must grab a hold of is that Jesus has our backs. We need to learn this as quickly as possible. Knowing and believing it will give us rest in our time of waiting for His answers to our questions.

To start a conversation with Jesus is as simple as talking to someone. You may not be looking at Him face-to-face, but the feeling He lets us experience of His presence is beyond the physical sight. When we draw near to God, the Word says He will then draw near to us. The Lord is the one with the plan for us, and we need those valuable seconds with Him to start finding out what those plans are. Longevity with God does not naturally produce long conversations with the Master. We can get too busy in ministry and forget the One who put us there. We start to rely on our own abilities that He blessed us with and forget to bring Him into our daily walks. We need to come back. We need to seek out our first love again, and that might mean starting over from the beginning, the type of beginning that starts out by saying, "Good morning, Lord."

The word says if we love Him, we will keep His word and that the Trinity will come and abide in us. Jesus truly wants to commune with us daily. Jesus will teach us what we need to know to prosper both here and in Heaven. Where we fall short is in us. We need to start out small and work big with Him who saves us. *The thief comes only to steal, kill, and destroy; I came that they may have life and have it abundantly* (John 10:10).

The Names of God

I would like to encourage you to take the time right now and go back and review the names I have written down. I periodically do this myself. I use them in my prayer time and when I worship Him. The better I know Him, the better I can converse with the One who knows me better than I know me. Remember He is Shammah, He is already there waiting for you. Now go, be with Him, and review

His precious names. I really encourage you to mark in your book. I hope to meet you one day and you can show me how the Lord has had you right down His epiphanies to you about these sentences.

Running the Race

Run, run, run, run, and run...that's what we are to do! We are called to win. It is what He desires. Heaven accepts no losers, because God only creates winners. The problem with that is we have to want to run the race; He will never force us. There are many things we can do to hedge our running a great race. Our spiritual clothing is paramount. We must only run with what we absolutely need and nothing more. As we pray each day, the Lord will make sure we are outfitted correctly. He, the Word, says will not leave us nor forsake us, so we need to stand on that promise. As we are running, we need to lay aside our old selves and put on the new selves. This new self will be in Christ a leaner, more eager to please servant who will have the desire to please the Living God.

Shoes are a part of the spiritual clothing and are greatly needed to run efficiently and fast. Shoes are the preparation of the gospel of peace and are highly needed to win. Please, as you receive the gospel of peace, tie it properly on your feet. Make it fit—you might have a long run.

As we run this race for Jesus, we need to run for His glory and not our own. Stay in tune with His every instruction. The Lord is the one who knows the route.

Who Is Your Verifier?

I pray that if you made it in the book this far, you made Jesus your one and only verifier. Since He created you, who best would know your needs and desires? I pray that the Word is becoming more real in your life. The Word is living, active, and sharper than any two-edged sword, so use it. The Word can divide the soul and spirit and thoughts and intensions of the heart. Which one of us can do that? We need the Word for our verification. We need a person who can make a rational decision for us based on our absolute needs, and the only one who can do that is Jesus. Sorry, not even our best friends can do that.

Jesus said to him, "I am the way, and the truth, and the life; no one comes to the Father but through Me" (John 14:6).

"Therefore everyone who hears these words of mine and acts on them may be compared to a wise man who built his house on the rock" (Matthew 7:24).

We need to remember that Jesus is the way, the truth, and the life, and the only way to the Father is through Him. Now that's a verifier. The Word tells us that if we hear the word and act on it, we are like a wise man who builds his house on a rock. Sounds like a good plan to me as long as we act on the word. I have built a house, and when we had the foundation poured, it was thicker than a normal house in the area, and it had more cement mixed in. We used a formula for maximum hardness. When we sold the house twenty-six years later, there was not one crack in the walls or foundation. Good planning calls for good measures taken. Who would want to build anything on sand anyway?

When we realize that there is really nothing we can do on our own initiatives, we learn to settle in and seek His guidance. We need this guidance daily, not weekly or monthly, but every day. Let Jesus be your daily verifier. He has all the answers to all your questions.

What Do You Smell Like?

We have learned from the scriptures that our prayers go up to the Lord as incense, a smell of sorts. We can, by our prayers, get God's attention with both nostrils. Smells are important to Him. How do you wish to smell? Do you want to be a sweet aroma to Him? Prayer is everything to our scent. Prayer gives off an aroma that either captures His attention or it doesn't.

When we go to Him in prayer with His will in mind, the fragrance on us is awesome, but when our prayers are not part of His plan, the fragrance diminishes greatly. Unforgiveness stagnates our fragrance, as it stops our prayers all together. When we pray from the heart and give knowing we will get nothing back, this confuses the enemy as he does not know how to stop it. The enemy cannot steal, kill, or destroy unselfish behavior.

We have learned that when you carry Christ with you wherever you go, you take with you a fragrance unto life. When you walk with the enemy, you carry a fragrance unto death. Which do you prefer? You have read in this book that prayer is not hard, and it does not have to be long, but it does have to be consistent. When we go to the Lord every day, we hear from Him every day. You may not realize it right away, but you are walking with Him and you are giving off a fragrance of life..

We are told to be imitators of God. Jesus gave us some fantastic examples that are not hard to follow. We do need, however, to walk in love. We must walk in His agape love. When we cannot walk in this kind of love, which is an unselfish love, we must ask Him for His help. We must remember that His grace is sufficient for all our needs and not just a few. Our responsibility is to go to Him. He has the plan, and we must find it out. When we do, we carry a fragrant aroma of life.

Really, when you think about it, why would you want to carry an offensive smell? Instead. carry a fragrant aroma that captures the attention of the Master.

Changing Your Harvest

We have the ability to change our harvests at any time. We will reap what we sow! Knowing these two things, wouldn't you want a harvest you can eat, sell, and replant for additional harvests? Yet we ignore our abilities. We chose to go on in life and not pay any attention to what we do and what we receive. No farmer can exist on one harvest. The farmer must replant if he wants to eat again. This principle of reseeding and getting multiple harvests should attract you. If you go about planting seed, you then can go about looking for your harvests. Always reinvest some of your seed. Do not eat it all, or you will have nothing to plant for your future.

I planted, Apollos watered, but God was causing the growth. So then neither the one who plants nor the one who waters is anything, but God who causes the growth (1 Corinthians3:6–7).

One thing I would like to remind you: no matter how talented you are, your seed comes from the Living God in all His generosity. As you water your seed, you must remember this also comes from Him. When your harvest comes in, again you must give Him thanks because it is by His mercy and grace you have a crop. Give of your first fruits to further the kingdom. You will be surprised what the Lord will do with 90 percent of your crop as opposed to 100 percent. I know it makes no sense whatsoever, but that is the God I serve. I can't speak for you, but as for me, I want the Lord, King, and Master that I serve to be able to defy what makes no sense and create victories for me. Out of nothing, comes something, Him ! If you want this too, you must be willing to go where He tells you, because He will send you to them. He will give you the Divine suddenlies. He will defy what the world says "cannot be," and He will make it happen for you.

Crossing Over

I know you just got through reading this chapter, and it is fresh in your mind so I won't belabor it. I do want to say that we as Christians must want this. We must desire to cross over from bondage to freedom for the new Christian, and crossing over from wandering to the promise for the older, perhaps more seasoned Christian. Please, do not give up. Do not let the enemy steal promises from you. Pursue Jesus with everything you have. Don't be afraid of the seven seconds with God. Let Him take you from a few seconds to new heights with Him. To cross over means you are exercising your faith. Awesome—do it! Crossing over means you will never be the same again.

Right now, wherever you are reading these last words to this book, ask Him! Ask Jesus to cross you over to the other side. If you have not truly accepted Him as Lord and savior, do it now! Don't wait one more second. Cross over from bondage of the world to freedom in Christ. Remember to embrace the cross, His shed blood for the remission of our sins, and the fact that the Father accepted Jesus sacrifice for us all.

If you are a seasoned Christian, and you have had many victories, and you have accomplished much but have lost your prayer time with the Master, stop! Get back to your first love, and if you don't, you will run out of spiritual gas. Sometimes we are allowed to go on our own, but it never lasts, and we end up crashing and burning. When this happens, and if it has happened to you already, remember our God is sufficient for all your needs. He will raise you up again as He did Abraham, Moses, and David. They kept going in the Lord. It is what raised them up again, and you must too. Get back to your quiet time with Jesus, and let Him breathe life back into your bones. Let Him put flesh back on your bones and the warrior fight back in your heart. He never leaves or forsakes us, but we do leave or forsake Him.

Get back in the race and back in the fight. The prize goes to the one who finishes the race.

My prayers for you are going out as you breathe. God is already taking you by the hand. Stand up and put on the full armor. The Psalms say that He prepares a table before you in the presence of your enemies, and this I know to be true. What I also know is that you must pull yourself up to the table in order to enjoy and receive what He has prepared. Do it! I know in Christ that you can.

To contact Dennis Eisch

If you have accepted Jesus while you were reading this book, or you are a pastor and want to get a hold of me for any reason, you can e-mail me at { deisaiah662@yahoo. com } our ministry is called "ISAIAH66:2 MINISTRIES LLC ,restoration through Christ Jesus. You can also facebook us at ISAIAH66.2 MINISTRIES.